# The Performer's Edge

### Different Thinking for Innovative Leaders

by Tobias Beckwith

*with Sylvia Brallier, Paul Draper, Kevin Lepine and Jeff McBride*

Triple Muse Publications

Copyright © 2025 by Toby L. Beckwith. All rights reserved.

No part of this book may be used or reproduced in any manner whatsoever without written permission except in the case of brief quotations embodied in critical articles and reviews.

For information, visit www.triplemusepublications.com
E-mail: tobias@wizardventure.com

FIRST EDITION

Book design and layout by Tobias Beckwith
www.tobiasbeckwith.com

Illustrations and Editing by Sylvia Brallier
www.sylviabrallierart.com

Published by Triple Muse Publications

Library of Congress Cataloging-in-Publication Data has been applied for.
ISBN 979-8-9926512-0-1

# Contents

## Introduction ......... 1
Art and Illusion ......... 2
Disillusionment ......... 3
Breaking Rules ......... 6
Reality Distortion ......... 8
Art and Business ......... 11
Help from my friends ......... 12

## Creating Reality ......... 15

## The Jumping Band ......... 19
Why it Works ......... 21

## Performers and Reality ......... 23
An Invisible Symphony:
Beyond the Walls of Perception ......... 25
A Conversation on Perception ......... 26
A Tourist's Mirage:
Decoding the Facades of Reality ......... 29
Distorting Perception:
The Magician's Playground ......... 31
A Sea of Mis-Perception ......... 33
A Prism of Perception ......... 34
Conscious vs. Subconscious ......... 37
The Art of Disguise ......... 44
Who Am I, Really? ......... 48

## Changing Culture to Change Reality .................. 51

The Maze of Identity:
Fear, Ritual, and the Power of Facing the Unthinkable .... 54

Disillusionment and the Power of Illusion:
From Stage Tricks to Life-Shaping Moments ................... 55

The Alchemy of Awe:
Transformational Moments ................................................ 58

Navigating the Moral Maze:
From Cute Lamb to Drone Warfare ................................. 60

## Story Power ........................................................ 65

## The Jumping Band Revisited ............................. 97

A Story with The Jumping Band ............................................ 99

## Creative vs. Competitive ................................... 103

Make it a Game! ....................................................................... 106

## Responsibility and Power .................................. 109

Radical Responsibility with Kevin Lepine ........................... 111

Owning your Venue ................................................................ 113

Getting Help Builds Your Power .......................................... 116

Emulating Success: A Ladder, Not a Leap .......................... 121

Embrace the "I'll Find Out" Ethos ....................................... 121

Beyond Price Tags: Cultivating Value ................................. 123

The Wisdom of Questions ..................................................... 124

The Power of Boundaries ....................................................... 125

## Becoming the Change ....................................... 129

Aligning Action with Belief ................................................... 129

Bridging the Gap: From Intention to Action ..................... 131

Reprogramming the Narrative:

A Hypnotherapist's Guide ............................................. 133
The Power of Repetition and Metaphor:
   A Journey to Self-Discovery............................................ 136
The Alchemy of Acting:
   Body, Mind, and the Expressive Whole ....................... 138
Embodiment and the Expressive Journey......................... 141
The Art of Attention:
   Cultivating Mindfulness in Daily Life ........................... 143
The Alchemy of Success:
   Setting Goals and Embracing the Mission .................... 145
The Power of Why:
   Uncovering the Soul of a Mission ................................. 148
The Art of Listening: A Vital Link to Success ................... 151
Getting Into Character From the Outside In.................... 152
Trauma as Change Agent.................................................. 156
Performing is Story Telling ............................................... 158
The Magic of Mindset ....................................................... 160

# Question Everything! ........................................... 163
Questioning Beliefs and Assumptions............................... 163
Questioning Your Assumptions with Magic..................... 164
Feynman's Computing Team ............................................ 167
More Magicians' Secrets .................................................... 168
Reflection and Questioning............................................... 170

# Different Perspective, Different Reality ......... 173
A Bizarre Experience ........................................................ 173

# Attention is Everything..................................... 177
An Experiment in Directing Attention ............................. 178

## Practice is a Super Power ... 183
Rehearsal ... 184
Write Your Own Script ... 187
Practice for a Better Speaking Voice ... 188
A Conversation with Jeff McBride ... 189
Movement and Memory ... 203

## Conclusion ... 207
Point-by-Point Summary ... 207
Think Different ... 208

## Index ... 213

## Acknowledgments ... 215

## Follow Up ... 215
Other Books by Tobias Beckwith ... 215

# Introduction

Feeling powerless? Many of us do, many times a day. We get treated unfairly, or have difficulty making enough money to make ends meet. We see others with influential, fun friends, but can't get into those circles. We feel powerless in the face of authority of all kinds. It's frustrating! So, let's do something about it. I wrote this book for us!

Much of that powerless feeling we all hate comes from our acceptance of certain beliefs, certain roles that others have thrust upon us. But when we learn new ways of thinking, we can overcome those limiting beliefs. We can learn to think and act in more powerful ways. We can learn to become the leaders who create positive change in the world.

I come from a world outside what most would think of as normal business. For many years I worked as a manager and producer for productions and theaters in New York City, and then moved on to working with some of the world's top magicians as producer, director and business manager. The product was live entertainment — an experience that is by its very nature ephemeral. We sell creativity in its rawest, most fleeting form. Our lessons learned are not the usual lessons one might learn from running a more traditional business. It's this "counter intuitive" wisdom I have to offer here. Steve Jobs told us to "Think Different." I'm here to show you a few ways I've learned, from my own experience, that you can do that.

All business today is about providing experiences. We provide experiences for our customers, as well as for our employees. It's not just the physical products you might produce or sell, but the way that product makes a customer feel when they are buying and using it. If you're going to be a great leader in business today, you need to be able to construct wonderful experiences for everyone who comes in contact with the company. The experience you provide is your company's identity, as far as the world is concerned.

We all need to become experience designers. In show business, every new show is a new business — a startup, if you will. And as artists of the theater, creating special, transformation experiences is our business.

In the theater, we don't expect shows to last forever. The very nature of theater is that it is ephemeral. A show starts, runs for 90 minutes or 2 hours, and then it ends. The run of a show might be for a few months or a few years, but nothing runs forever. A show is also a kind of system. There is a story, a script, a number of actors, setting, lighting, costumes, venue, and, of course, an audience. That audience is in a particular city, country and culture. Each and every one of these factors has an effect on that show. The show affects the culture, and the culture affects the show. And it's the same for your business.

As the pace of change has accelerated in recent years, it seems that all businesses are becoming more like the theater business, in that respect. And as leaders of those businesses, there are lessons to learn from the artists.

I love this quote, originally attributed to Vivian Greene, that "Life isn't about waiting for the storm to pass. It's about learning how to dance in the rain."

It seems particularly relevant in these fast changing times.

## Art and Illusion

Have you ever wondered, what are the arts really for?

There are, of course, many answers. If you love comedy television, you might respond that they are for entertaining—a respite from the stressful and mundane. Do you love to visit art museums? Painting, photography, and sculpture are all there—for what purpose? To make us look at our world in different ways? To reproduce the beauty inherent in nature and thus call it to our attention?

Perhaps you enjoy music—classical, country, pop, or jazz. What do you get out of listening, or attending a concert? What aspect of your life outside the arts does that enhance? That one is tougher to put into words, at least for me. Most art imitates something, provides us a different way of looking at some experience from the "real world." But what does music imitate? It certainly makes us feel emotion, to relate to the world of movement in time, to get in touch with our emotions more directly than most other art forms. I'm not sure how to explain

## Introduction

the value that music brings to my life, but I know I'd certainly miss it if it were gone.

Perhaps making art is a way of sharing our various experiences of reality in ways that enrich those experiences for all who encounter the art. A way of celebrating the fact that human life is, or can be, more than just the animal necessities of food, drink, sex, and safety. Perhaps it is a way of expanding and enriching what it can mean to be human. Perhaps it is a way of rebelling against the false fetters our culture puts upon us.

In many ways, all of our experience is an illusion, create partly from the data our senses bring us about the outside world, but also from our existing beliefs, knowledge and assumptions. When that illusion is suddenly shattered — heartbreak! Just maybe, the arts are our way of re-creating reality without the restrictions of what our senses tell us must be true, and without the restrictions of the beliefs our culture has installed in us. Perhaps the arts, in their many manifestations, are all forms of magic, ways of "re-illusioning" our worlds.

## Disillusionment

> *"I knew nothing but shadows and I thought them to be real."*
> From Oscar Wilde's
> *The Picture of Dorian Grey*

My first great disillusionment came when I opened the first book I ever purchased. I was six years old at the time and had just learned to read. I already knew what interested me: Magic! My parents used to read bedtime stories to us, many of which included wizards and witches and feats of magic. "Of course, magic isn't real, except in stories," they told me. I didn't believe them.

I was beyond excited when our teacher offered us, hidden among many other "First Book of" offerings—things like sports, gardening, horses, sewing, and fifty other mundane subjects—a *First Book of Magic*. And it was for sale!

Here was my confirmation. Maybe magic was real! And here, hidden amongst the other "First Books," was my chance to learn about it. I ordered the book.

We filled in our forms, delivered our three-dollar payments to the teacher, and she sent the orders in for the whole class. Everyone was filled with anticipation, each having ordered a book about whatever interested them most. Looking back, this was a clever strategy by our teacher. Now that we could read, here was a great reason to become more involved—the chance to learn things we each really wanted to know, but that wouldn't be taught in classes. It certainly worked on me.

Weeks later, the books arrived, and we could hardly contain our excitement. No one else had thought to order the magic book, and I was certain I would be the only one privy to secret spells, potions, and other ways of wielding power. While my classmates eagerly showed each other their new treasures, I hid my book in my lap, almost under the desk, so no one else would know I had it.

I had plans for the magic I would learn. No more rainy days when I wanted to go outside to play, just to begin with. I'd have the power to put an end to that! And I'd make sure I could now run faster than any of my friends (I was far from the fastest). At last, I could be the master of my universe! I wrapped the book back in the brown paper it had come in and ran all the way home after school.

Barely taking time to let my mother know I was home, I rushed up the stairs, closed the door to my bedroom, and sat on the bed with my new treasure. I was a bit confused by the image on the cover. It showed a top hat and a magician's wand—that black cylinder with white caps on the ends. At the time, I hadn't seen a performing magician, and this was not my idea of what Merlin's tools would look like. Still...

I cracked the book open, smoothed the pages the way our teacher had showed us—and that's when it happened. My first big moment of disillusionment, disappointment, and heartbreak.

## Introduction

Oh, it started off well, with the number-one "rule of magic," which was "Never reveal your secrets." That made sense to my six-year-old ego. Keep that power for yourself. Keep it a secret!

But what followed was, well, probably the biggest disappointment of my life until that point. The book was just a description of a dozen or so tricks, tricks you could use to deceive your friends. There were tricks with pieces of string, salt shakers, Life Savers, and playing cards. Not a bit of real magic to be found! No wonderful mysterious powers, just a bunch of stupid tricks! You could create the illusion of pulling a string through your neck, or of taking a Life Saver off of a string without breaking it while your friend was holding both ends. You could cut a thread into several pieces, and then pretend to make it whole again. If you practiced enough, you could learn to do these things in a way that your friends might believe you had real powers—but no real powers were revealed. I was devastated!

We were required to do a book report in class on our new books, so I learned to perform two or three of the tricks in the book. Telling the class I wasn't allowed to reveal the secrets of how these things were done, but could show them the results, I performed several of them as part of my report. Looking back, I imagine that was my first time in front of an audience, and I was apprehensive. I didn't believe the tricks would actually deceive anyone, or that anyone would even be amused, except at my failure and naïveté for expecting more than the book could deliver.

But I was wrong. That first performance won me an A, and turned out to be the first of many times I've enjoyed performing for audiences of all kinds. I was unaware that the magic had worked, but it had worked to change me in a way I couldn't have anticipated.

Those early performances as a boy magician helped build a real love of performing, and I went on to study acting, performed music in several bands, and more. But the sense of disillusionment lingered. Magic was just tricks, and I still wanted it to be real! My love of performing led me to a career in the theater—I told myself there was more real magic, more ability to inspire wonder and create real transformations in a Broadway musical or film, than in any performance of tricks or illusions.

Somehow, though, I found my way back to performance magic, and, over the years, got to work extensively with some of the greatest magicians of my time. Even then, it took me several decades to come to the revelation that a magician's performance could be the source of real transformations in audiences. Tricks, and the special kinds of stories they created within the minds of audiences, could cause a change of mind, a change of belief—and that could change the world. Maybe magic is real—just not quite in the way my six-year-old self had believed!

## Breaking Rules

This book is my way of breaking that "first rule" not to reveal my secrets. Why? Because, like my friend Jeff McBride, I believe that we all have the potential to be magicians, and to re-create the reality of our own lives. I believe each of us deserves the ability to double down on who we really are and take advantage of our full potential as human beings. When we leave our limiting beliefs behind, when we learn to accept our real personal power, we each have the power to create a better world.

Our culture and education within that culture tends to limit us. But when you learn to shatter the illusions that hold you back, when you learn to see the world in new and different ways, nothing is impossible. This simple revelation can give you amazing powers within the context of your life, your business, and your community.

For me, one illusion was broken, only to be replaced later by a new one. We're often distressed when one of our cherished illusions falls apart — but it pays to remember there's a new, and probably better one coming to replace it.

There are problems, of course. We hate letting go of our cherished illusions. Change is often difficult and scary. We love our comforts and hate doing things that might endanger them. Change is work, and sometimes painful—except when it's fun! Taking control of our

## Introduction

own minds is a way to make it fun, and that's real magic. So let the fun begin!

Here's an example: I live in the US, where we purport to believe in and celebrate our "freedom." We hear that we "live in the land of the free" so many times we could hardly not believe it!

But few of us ever ask ourselves "are we really free?" I suppose, in order to answer that, you need to be able to define what is "freedom?" Free to do anything you want? Certainly not. We're not free to steal, kill, or disobey the traffic laws. We like living in a country with boundaries set by the rule of law. But some of us break those laws, and we are free to do so – as long as we're willing to pay the price for our transgressions by paying fines or going to jail.

So, are we free to do what we want within the law? I'd guess that's the general intent contained within the founding papers of our country, the Declaration of Independence and Constitution and Bill of Rights. The statement is that "All men are endowed by their Creator with certain unalienable Rights. Among these unalienable rights are Life, Liberty, and the pursuit of Happiness."

But if we're honest, we all know that form of liberty meant, and still means, vastly different things depending on how rich or poor you might be, what sex, religion and gender might be yours, and what level of education you have. These things limit each one of us in different ways depending on the part of the world, the time, and the culture that we live in.

Mohandas Gandhi once suggested that "no one can make you a slave without your permission." The truth is that we each enslave ourselves within the prisons of our own minds. Our parents, society, schools all come with a set of ideas about who and what we are and can be, and we tend to accept and believe those ideas, largely without questioning. Many of those beliefs limit our freedom and dis-empower us.

We tell ourselves things like "I could never do that," and believe it. Or things like, "that's not my responsibility." We wonder how the people who really change the world, who succeed in business or in the arts, are somehow specially gifted, and why we ourselves seem not to be.

I'm no different in this.

For many years, I knew I had done everything in my power to become a "total artist" of the theater, and positioned myself to become a Broadway producer. I learned to act, direct, design and build sets, lighting and costumes. I became a director, designer and theater manager.

"I can do everything but raise money," I told myself over and over, knowing full well that raising money was one of the core tasks of a producer. But I told myself I couldn't do that, because I didn't know rich people who could afford to invest — and so I never tried!

Decades later I attended pitch meet-ups in San Francisco, where tech startups introduced themselves to potential investors, and it occurred to me then that I could, in fact, raise money. I met dozens of potential venture capitalists, all eager to find ventures where they could invest their money. Not only could I find them, but they were eager to be found! I actually helped several rising entrepreneurs perfect their pitches and win funding. I couldn't do it for myself only because I believed that I could not!

Which brings me to the whole point of this book: The things you believe are impossible — for you, for your company, for your friends and family – are probably very possible, once you allow yourself to believe that they are. But you have to be willing to change yourself and your thinking.

*"To achieve the impossible; it is precisely the unthinkable that must be thought."*

from *Jitterbug Perfume* by Tom Robbins

## Reality Distortion

Both Steve Jobs and Bill Clinton were famous amongst those who worked with them for what was termed their "reality distortion fields." Jobs would ask employees to do something in a particular way, or within a particular time frame, which the employees were quite certain was impossible.

## *Introduction*

In one instance, Jobs wanted a prototype of the first iPod in one week, but was told there was no reality in which it could happen in less than 6 weeks. His engineers — the best in the business, mind you — laid out the whole process that would be necessary, and showed how they were having to cut corners just to achieve it within that 6 week time frame. "One week," he said, "or don't come to work again the week after that." The prototype was on his desk in one week. Reality, as it turns out, can be altered when you have enough motivation, and learn to believe that it can be.

Clinton, on the other hand, was famous for winning over his enemies just through his riveting personal presence. There was a New York Times Magazine profile which referred to his facility for "making eye contact so deep that recipients sometimes seem mesmerized. Tabloid rumors aside, Clinton embodies the parallels between the seductions of politics and the seductions of sex. As one Clinton watcher said recently: 'It's not that Clinton seduces women. It's that he seduces everyone.'"

But how do we go about changing the beliefs that we use to create the reality we live in? That's where we get back to the arts. Artists are tasked with exactly that job: Create imaginary realities in the form of graphic art, dramatic art, novels (especially science fiction!), music and more, which stretch our ideas and beliefs of what possible reality is and can be.

The arts — especially the performing arts — allow us to share our experiences of life with more intensity and focus than we can in the real world – but without the fear and pain that we might experience in "real life." You can always close a book or walk out of a movie. And yet, the stories told, the feelings engendered, the beliefs expressed, change us almost as though we had gone through the "real" experiences. Those who create those "imaginary" experiences must often learn skills and techniques that would be extremely useful to those of us who don't think of ourselves as artists, but as workers, executives, parents, etc.

Where most of us believe it takes weeks and months or longer to change ourselves – to build a better body, sharpen our minds, learn new skills, etc. – actors learn to transform themselves very quickly. Dustin here can transform himself into Tootsie with just two or three hours of getting into makeup, costume, and – most of all – into character. What's his secret? I'll tell you more about it later on in the book, but just a hint – it's something you can learn, too, and put to use in your life.

I've spent much of the last 40 years working with top performing magicians like Jeff McBride, Marco Tempest and Paul Draper, helping them build their shows, curate their public images, and use the tools of magic and illusion to create entertaining and enlightening theatrical shows. Magic is the one form of theater that relies, not on a suspension of disbelief, but on its opposite. You must believe the "reality" the magician presents ("this is just a normal deck of playing cards") in order to experience that reality being transformed. Magicians count on their audiences to rely on their beliefs, and we manipulate those beliefs in order to fool them into seeing things that are actually (they believe) impossible.

Magicians learn the importance of directing an audience's attention. They are adept at disguising objects as other objects, actions as other actions, and taking advantage of an audiences' particular point of view. Most of all, they take advantage of the fact that our experiential reality is created mostly within our minds, based on assumptions, prior learning and beliefs — and doesn't always correspond with the world that is actually "out there."

Performing magic leads us to the understanding that we all rely on assumptions about the world in order to create our experienced reality, and that brings us to the realization that in many ways, it's all an illusion. We'll discuss this at length in the next chapter.

Every one of us has the same capabilities to distort reality as those stage magicians do, once we know their secrets. Just like Jobs and Clinton, we can distort — and actually change — the reality that we and those around us experience, if we have the will to do so. All we really need is that will and the "secret knowledge" of the artists who already do it every day.

## Introduction

## Art and Business

*"Change your thoughts and you change your world."*
- Norman Vincent Peale

I know – this all smacks a bit of hocus pocus and the supernatural. You're right to be skeptical.

But changing minds is the task of artists of all a kinds. The novelist creating imaginary worlds and inviting us to come into those worlds – they are providing us with experiences that change our view of the world around us. Actors transform themselves before our eyes, and invite us to "live vicariously" through their exploits on stage and screen. Graphic artists distill or distort the images of the world around us, and make us appreciate things differently. Artists are all in the business of changing individuals and cultures.

Here's the kicker: This is also what we are about when we create a new business. We have to look at the culture (market) we live in, and see how we think it should to change. (This can be as simple and mundane as, "I'd love not having to drive so far for my donuts every day — maybe I need to open a donut shop near me.") We have to create ways (our products) for that change to take place. We have to inspire our teams, reach out and get our potential market to imagine and understand how their reality will be better when they use our products. And, once some of them begin to do just that, we have to observe and listen to their reactions in order to see if we are succeeding, or if we need to change what we're doing until we do. When that works, we have to spread the story of how and why it works, and how lives are changing. In this sense, every entrepreneur needs to be as much a creative artist as David Copperfield, Stephen King or James Cameron.

In the following pages you'll find discussions with some of my favorite thinkers from the worlds of magic, healing arts, science and more. Subjects include why, in many ways, our experience is all illusion – and then how we can each become a grand illusionist, an artist of life, capable of creating our own reality distortion fields, with the ability to actually create change in our lives, businesses and the world around us.

Concepts include the directive to question everything, especially our own experienced reality. Why do we see, hear, experience the world we live in as we do? If bats and dolphins can hear shapes and distances – why can't we? If bees can dance to show one another where the best flowers found are, why not humans? Another directive is to learn to consider things from many different perspectives. Yet another is to learn to see things as a systems expert would. We can view ourselves as tiny systems, made up of even tinier systems and living within larger systems, which in turn exist in even larger systems. How can we learn to become aware of all of these systems, and to create the small changes in one that will effect larger changes in all? How can we learn to view every situation in all these different ways, and if we do, how will that empower us?

How can the secrets of actors and magicians, specifically help us through all this?

It's hard letting go of our old illusions – but when you realize you have the power to create new, bigger and better illusions, and live those out — that's exciting! If I hadn't experienced that first disillusionment with my book of magic tricks, I would never have searched out all these different ways of thought — and the ability to create real magic.

## Help from my friends

Some people have sometimes suggested that I would be better off shifting my life away from the "frivolous" pursuits of the arts that have delighted and supported for the past 50 years. A transition towards something more practical like business, finance, or law would make sense, as far as they are concerned. Yet, how could I abandon this world of creativity that so nourishes my soul? The arts are not mere ornaments, but, at least for me, the very essence of what makes us human. I'm happy that several of my favorite human artists have agreed to join me for some of the discussions that follow.

You'll meet my friend **Paul Draper** in just a bit. Paul is an entertainer – magician, mentalist, and keynote speaker. He's also a cultural anthropologist, consultant and college lecturer. He can amaze you by telling you things about yourself you wouldn't think he could know,

## Introduction

predicting choices you'll make before you've made them, and more. He can also help you understand how you, too, can read others, break out of limitations you've imposed on yourself, and much more.

**Sylvia Brallier** has spent most of her career investigating phenomena that some might think of as being real magic. Somatic healing practices, transformational breath practices, hypnotherapy, and the use of trance states to help others access their true potential are a few of the areas where her first-hand expertise will lead us.

**Kevin Lepine** headlines his own show, Hypnosis Unleashed, in Las Vegas. It's unlike any other hypnosis show you might have encountered. Kevin shares his thoughts on what it's like to take the "ultimate responsibility" for a dozen or more volunteers who hand themselves over for the hypnotic experience he provides them — in front of large audiences made up of friends, family, and complete strangers — every night! Kevin has reinvented himself over and over again throughout his life, and he shares some of his experience doing that.

Finally, my longtime friend and partner in so many different shows and enterprises I can no longer name all of them is **Jeff McBride.** Initially drawn together in order to create theatrical shows using Jeff's unique combination of martial arts, pantomime, Kabuki theater and some of the best and most dynamic sleight-of-hand performances ever, we went on to build large shows for the casino and corporate theater market. We toured a variety of magic and illusion shows internationally. In the early 1990s we launched the McBride Magic & Mystery School, which has become the premiere school for magicians in the world. Jeff's insights on the magic of practice and rehearsal below are invaluable, not just for performers, but for anyone interested in pursuing excellence in any field.

There may be things in the pages ahead that make you uncomfortable when you first read them, but I hope you'll bear with me, and see where those uncomfortable thoughts can take you. I read a media posting recently: "All of your dreams lie just outside your comfort zone." So I invite you on this journey, and hope it leaves you feeling empowered. Empowered to create the changes in your life, in your organization – in the world – that the world so desperately needs!

# Chapter 1
# Creating Reality

Several years ago, my friend Marco Tempest was working on a performance piece which would become his next TED talk. It was a piece in which he collaborated on stage with a large humanoid robot – to do magic! Marco had purchased an early version of the Baxter Manufacturing Robot. Advertised as a robot that, unlike traditional robots, which are programmed to follow a specific set of commands, Baxter could be programmed by moving its hand to perform a task whose motions the computer will then memorize and be able to repeat; as such, the bot could be programmed by ordinary workers, without the need of an expert being present. The reality wasn't quite that.

So, Marco, then a Director's Fellow at the MIT Media Lab, hired a team of roboticists to help him program his Baxter to do the magic routine he wanted to show.

(You can see the final routine on the TED site: https://www.ted.com/talks/marco_tempest_and_for_my_next_trick_a_robot?subtitle=en)

I remember speaking with Marco one day, from his MagicLab space in New York, and he explained some of the difficulties he was having in creating the special programming for the robot.

"It's not just the kind of easy "If this, then that" you usually encounter when you're programming."

"So, what's so different?"

"Well, the robot has all these sensors. Cameras, touch sensors, microphones, etc. So it's almost like a person, taking in many streams of data which it converts into an internal model of reality. As the human working with the robot, I become part of that model. To learn the routine, the robot responds to its model, not directly to the sensors. It wants to move its arm in a certain way, so first it senses where the arm is now, then adds that to it's internal model, figures where and how it wants to move the arm, then sends out the message to the actuators in that arm to move, and creates a new version of its model.

At the same time, certain sensors do create immediate responses, like our reflexes do, so that the robot won't actually hurt me if I get in the way. It's kind of a complicated process getting the input, creating the model, and then deciding the next step and programming the movements of the model, with its imaginary hands, facial expressions, and so on. And all that has to happen in milliseconds."

A few years later I picked up a book called The Mind Has a Body of its Own, by Sandra & Matthew Blakeslee. The book explained that our minds are constructed very much as Marco's robot was. We take in input from our senses, which send many streams of data – visual, aural, touch, etc. – and combine them, along with learned knowledge and previously held beliefs, to create a model of both our external and internal realities. The model exists only within our brains. And, like the robot, that model is what we experience as our "reality," and what we use when we interact with the outside world.

More recently, I saw a TED talk by Donald Hoffman, inquiring "Do we see reality as it is?" in which Professor Hoffman makes much the same case: The reality we experience is mostly created within our minds. Sure, there's some kind of reality "out there," but our senses are only designed to pick up a small part of what's there. Evolution designed us to survive – not to understand the grand scheme of reality. What we experience as "reality," then, is largely an illusion.

Perhaps, more accurately, it is a sequence of illusions, much in the way a film is a sequence of images, which when played at a certain rate, create the sensation of continuity. Our minds have to recreate that whole illusion of reality at least 20 times or so every second in order to avoid that flickering sensation you might have noticed when seeing an old movie, or flipping through a flip-book animation. It's amazing that our minds can do it at all, and still have time to think about anything beyond the split-second of reality we're experiencing right now!

In the words of scientist and explorer J.B.S. Haldane, "Reality isn't just stranger than you imagine. It's stranger than you can imagine!" Why? Because our minds are limited, and designed to understand only what we need to in order to survive. Our senses are limited – our eyes pick up about 1% of the electromagnetic spectrum. Ears hear sounds

## Chapter 1 - Creating Reality

within the frequency range of approximately 20 Hz to 20,000 Hz (20 kHz) under normal conditions. Our other senses are similarly limited, and it's tough to understand elements of what's out there when it's outside your ability to even sense it.

Think of it this way: Bats and dolphins live in a reality where they can hear shapes and distances. Bees see patterns in UV which tell them vastly more about the flowers where they gather pollen than we can see. Your dog can hear sounds well above the 20 kHz that you hear. Each of these creatures experiences a vastly different reality from the one you and I do.

The reality experienced is even significantly different from one human being to the next. If you have good color sense, you see a different world than the one I see. I have red-green color blindness, also known as deuteranomaly. So the colors you experience are different than the ones I do. Similarly, if you're sitting on the other side of the room and something happens in the space between us, you experience a different reality than the one I do, just because we're seeing it from different angles. If I'm involved in a conversation with a friend, and something happens across the room, I have a different experience of that event than someone who is watching it directly and without distraction. The "out there" reality might be the same, but our experienced realities are quite different.

Our brains are trained and tuned to experience – or, better, to create – a model of reality based on our sensory capabilities. Because we have achieved consciousness, we are led to wonder how and why things happen – and thus move beyond the simple reality our senses and minds create for us. We use science to figure out things about the reality outside our direct experience — but we tend not to experience those varieties of reality in the same immediate way that we do within what we might term "normal" reality.

We can enhance our natural senses — if we put on night vision goggles, which transform infrared light into images, we see the heat signatures of objects around us. Other instruments detect vibrations we can't feel directly, scents we can't smell, etc., and translate those into versions of reality that we can experience. Imagine the different realities we might create for ourselves if our senses were attuned to X-rays or gamma rays!

Let's take this all a bit further. Let's look at how we experience reality through time.

How do you remember things that have happened to you? You can remember that walk you took in the park this morning, or the interaction you had with the barista at your coffee shop – but how? Think about it now. Take a moment to remember and recreate some recent, simple experience you've had. It may be useful to write it down. Keep it short, like this:

"I opened the door to the coffee shop, and let my dog walk in before I did. There were two young women at the table nearest the door, and they saw the dog and reacted. "What a cutie," one of them said. I walked over the counter and said hello to the barista waiting for me there…"

You get the idea. As I recall the experience from memory, what I'm really recalling is a sequence of the "reality moments" that I experienced and paid attention to when they were taking place. My brain actually stored only bits and pieces, but my mind fills in the details – sometimes accurately, but often not. As I relate that experience here, I'm reliving the sequence in my mind. I somehow know that it's not actually happening again, and yet I'm experiencing it again, on some level. The recalled experience is not as rich, not as filled with every sense element and emotion as the original experience was. What I'm really doing is telling myself a story.

Stories, as it turns out, are super important. They are how we make sense of the reality model that we've created. We'll be talking a lot about stories in the coming pages. But first, let's have some fun and learn a simple magic trick.

# Chapter 2
# The Jumping Band

This is probably the first magic trick many young people learn. I'm teaching it to you here in order to show how easy it is to distort reality, for yourself and others. You'll need a rubber band, or, better, a small hair tie. That's all you need. You can buy a bag of 30 hair-ties at a Dollar Store for $1.25, and you're set to do this trick forever. In this chapter, you'll only need one of the bands, and your hands.

Hold up one hand with the palm facing your audience. Make that Vulcan "Live long and prosper" sign, with your index and 2nd fingers together, a space, and then your ring finger and pinky together. It should look like a V. Lower your hand so you're looking at the back of it. Use your other hand to place the band around the index and middle fingers. (It needs to be big enough to go easily around two fingers, and able to stretch to go around all four) Let your fingers all come together, then make a fist, and notice the situation. This is what you'll show your friend first when you show the trick.

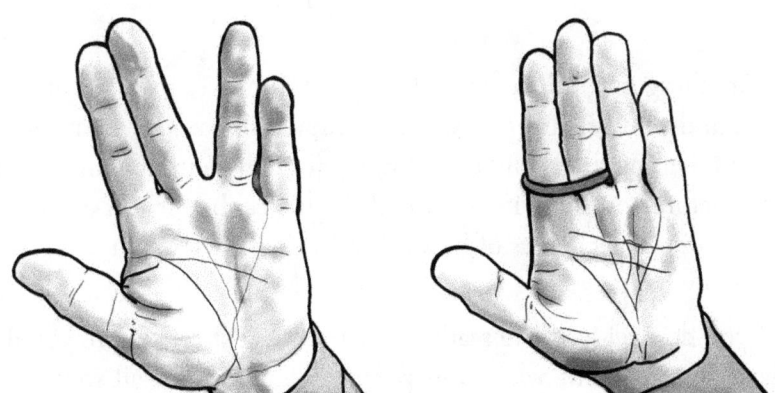

Now, loosen your fist, and turn your hand so that you can grab the band from the inside of your hand (using the other hand) and stretch it around the outside of all four fingers, inside the fist. The view on the outside (upper side) of the fist won't change, and you're not going to show this situation inside the fist to anyone. Turn the fist again, so the palm is down and your knuckles facing up.

When I show this trick, I like to raise the fist slightly and count "one," as I bring it back down to level. Then again, to count "two." I raise it one last time, count "three" as I bring it down and extend the fingers so the hand is now open and flat, with the back of the hand still upwards.

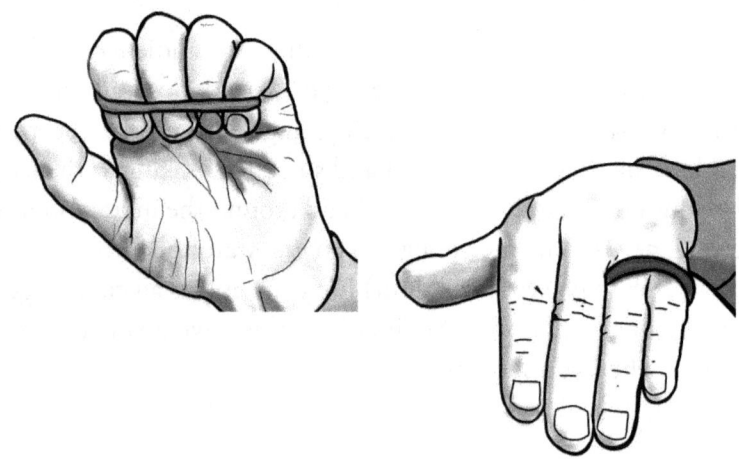

Something magical happens. That band, firmly in place around your index and middle fingers, has now jumped off those two and is now around the ring finger and pinky! Enjoy fooling yourself with this a few times before you show it to a friend. Don't feel bad if you don't figure out the exact mechanics of how it works the first few times you do it. Just enjoy the magic!

If you do decide you're ready to share this, just make sure you don't "flash" the moment when you put the band around all four fingers inside the fist. I do it by turning the back of my hand to the audience, held upright, and give a tug on the band from the inside, saying, "Just notice how it's nice and snug around those fingers." At that point, I close the fingers and wrap the band around the inside as I'm turning

## Chapter 2 - The Jumping

it palm down again, showing the band in place and getting ready for the 1-2-3 jump moment. If you want, you can use that same move to make it jump back to the initial position.

I suggest you get some kind of rubber band or small hair tie and play with this for a few minutes before we break it down and use it to demonstrate how we're using basic magic mechanics to bend reality. Have fun!

## Why it Works

So what are the lessons we have to learn from the Jumping Band trick?

First: How does it fool us? For me, the first way is by managing our point of view, our perspective. If you look at the trick from the angle the audience sees, you see the band jump magically from two fingers to two others. It appears to pass right through — solid through solid. But if you turn your fist so the palm is up, you see something quite different. The effect is still a bit counterintuitive, but you realize almost immediately that the bands are going around the tips of the fingers and onto the other fingers. It looks clever, but not impossible. Solids are not passing through one another at all, even though, from the other perspective, they would seem to do so.

Second: Because we tell our audience that what they're seeing is magical, that the band will magically jump from one position to another, they're not really thinking about the fact that something else is actually going on. We're directing their attention in such a way that they will see what we want them to.

Third: The band moves fast. If you just watch it intently without anything else moving, you can see it go. However, those slight moves of the hand up and down as I count "3, 2, 1, Go!" are larger movements, and our minds are distracted by those larger movements, not noticing the smaller one at all.

So, the lesson here is this: Control someone's attention and perspective (point of view), and you can control their perceived reality. By the same token, when you want to practice questioning everything in the world around you, ask yourself what something might look like from a different perspective. Make yourself notice the parts of things you might not be paying attention to. Just as we can influence others this way, we can also expand our own sense of reality and of what is actually possible.

This wraps it up for The Jumping Band for now, but I'll teach you how to make this a much stronger experience for yourself and whoever you show it in a couple of more chapters. In the meantime, have fun sharing this with your friends. The more you do it, the more deceptive it will become.

# Chapter 3
# Performers and Reality

Let's explore this idea of reality from a slightly different perspective, one in which we assume a unique vantage point — that of performing magicians and actors. These are artists who perceive the world through a set of lenses that sets them apart from most of the rest of us. Within their craft, these artists come to comprehend a fundamental truth about reality — that it is not singular but manifold – with a different version experienced by the performers than the one experienced by their audiences.

For the conjurer on stage, reality takes on a peculiar duality — sometimes, even plurality. They stand in the spotlight, donning their role as an enchanter who holds a key to unseen realms. Imagine the magician displaying a fan of three cards to their spectators — but with the knowledge of a fourth concealed behind the others. That single card, combined with the magician's dexterity and ability to create a narrative, becomes a tool for conjuring marvels. The magician has to keep track of both the audience's version of reality, and the magician's own, in which he must manipulate that additional card.

In contrast, the audience beholds a singular reality, entwined with the narrative spun by the magician. They are captivated by the tale the magician weaves, blissfully unaware of the unseen forces at play. The conjurer crafts an illusion, orchestrating perceptions that leave the audience immersed in a tale of wonder, never aware of the reality behind the scenes.

This notion of multiple realities isn't limited to magicians, but reaches into every corner of our lives – say, the marketing efforts of a big oil company, a giant retail behemoth, or even a popular celebrity. These entities also navigate the territory of selective reality.

My friend Paul Draper and I recently discussed some of the various ways this multiplicity of experienced realities can affect our world and, more importantly for the purposes of this book, our ability to create change using this knowledge.

Paul is a cultural anthropologist who studies consciousness, belief, and culture. He is also an internationally recognized mentalist, magician and speaker who has headlined in Las Vegas, off Broadway, and at celebrated, star-studded events all around the globe. I hope you'll find our conversation below as stimulating as I did.

> *Tobias Beckwith: Our subject here is how each one of us creates our own reality, based partly on what's out there, partly on what we pay attention to, and partly to the beliefs and knowledge we've collected.*
>
> *Paul Draper: I'd like to approach the whole thing from a slightly different perspective. I recently visited a zoo, and found myself contemplating the intricacies of intelligence prompted by a conversation I had with a koala bear expert. I learned of a brain scan revealing that the koala's cerebral surface is as smooth as a cue ball. We've known for a long time that there is a direct correlation between intelligence and brain surface area, with human brains showing deep folds in order to take maximum advantage of the area available.*
>
> *As my companion and I discussed the implications of this revelation, a question arose: Is a koala inherently less intelligent due to its seemingly limited cerebral landscape? The expert's response was that a koala is exactly as intelligent as is required to be a koala. This observation would also seem to apply to intelligence in human beings.*
>
> *Tobias: Am I hearing you say that we are as smart as is necessary to fulfill our roles as human beings? This tailored intelligence shapes our perception, reactions, and the very reality we inhabit. Much like the koala's specialized cognition, our human experience is finely tuned to the necessities of human survival. Is that right?*
>
> *Paul: Yet, there seems to be a difference. Unlike koalas, who experience reality within the parameters of their survival needs, human beings possess an innate curiosity and a drive to expand their understanding.*

## Chapter 3 - Performers and Reality

*This intrinsic human inclination leads us to construct instruments such as telescopes in outer space and microscopes in labs, instruments that reach beyond the restrictions of our natural senses. The act of building these tools reflects a profound desire to transcend our natural limitations. It is in this pursuit of knowledge, unbounded by immediate survival concerns, that human intelligence shines.*

*When we look at the world as a whole, the contrast between koalas and humans becomes apparent. While both species exhibit an intelligence tailored for their situations, humans possess an innate thirst for knowledge, extending beyond the necessities of survival. This dichotomy, encapsulated in our ability to build instruments for exploration, defines the unique trajectory of human intelligence— propelled by an insatiable curiosity to unravel the mysteries of the universe.*

## An Invisible Symphony:
## Beyond the Walls of Perception

*Human perception, tailored for our survival, but with that curious something extra, is certainly a fascinating phenomenon. We rely heavily on sight, yet it only grants us access to a tiny fragment of the electro-magnetic spectrum. Imagine the beauty we might perceive if our eyes were attuned to the ultraviolet light enjoyed by bees or the infrared worlds perceived by mosquitoes and snakes. What must it be like to experience the intricate echo-painted world navigated by dolphins? The realities they experience must be vastly different from the one you and I live in.*

Of course, there are people who claim that they do perceive more, who we are quick to dismiss because we believe their visions are unfounded, or because they seem to challenge the foundations of our understanding of reality. These are the mystics, psychics, faith healers and others. What if they are simply more attuned to the unseen forces that surround us, vibrations and energies that dance just beyond the grasp of our limited senses?

It is tempting to draw a hard line between the proven and the unproven, to label the unknown as mere fantasy or trickery. But perhaps the greatest magic lies not in dismissing these phenomena as acts of deception, but in the willingness to embrace the vastness of the unknown, to acknowledge the possibility that our current understanding represents only a single thread in a multi-layered reality.

As William James is purported to have written, "The greatest discovery of my generation is that human beings can alter their lives by altering their attitudes of mind." Perhaps it is time we cast aside some of our skepticism and embrace the potential for wonder that lies beyond the walls of our conscious perception.

## A Conversation on Perception

*Paul: It's clear that we humans recognize patterns that other creatures simply don't. And interestingly, our perception and ability to perceive new things changes as we age. When we're young, our brains are constantly learning and forming new connections, so we engage with the world in a much more exploratory way. But as we get older, our brains become more efficient at pattern matching, and we begin to categorize and label our experiences. We stop seeing each chair as a new and exciting object to explore, and instead recognize it simply as a "chair."*

*Tobias: Exactly. I think an interesting way to think about this is to consider the experience of a newborn baby. Their world is completely different from ours. There are no objects, no words, no concepts. It's a blur of color and noise, devoid of shapes and recognizable forms. Eventually, they start to notice recurring patterns, like mama's face, and from that, each of us begins to construct our own internal model of reality.*

*Paul: Right. We each start with a relatively clean slate.*

*Tobias: The world provides us with raw data, but it's up to our brains to interpret and organize that data into our individual versions of reality. This process of building our internal models is ongoing throughout our lives.*

*My friend Marco Tempest was once involved in creating a robot companion he could perform magic with. He explained to me*

## Chapter 3 - Performers and Reality

*that robots need to develop both reflexes for immediate responses – at least in part so they won't hurt those around them — and a complete internal model of their own bodies and surroundings if they are to function effectively. To accomplish things in the world, the robot brain interfaces with its internal model directly, and that model controls its actions in the outer world. By creating the model, which is far less detailed and complex than what is really "out there," the robot's "brain" can handle and function within the simpler reality it has created.*

*Paul: So the robot becomes aware of itself as an entity within the world.*

*Tobias: In a way. And just like a robot, we are constantly refining our understanding – our internal models — of ourselves and the world around us. This ongoing process of perception and interpretation shapes our experiences and contributes to the unique way each of us navigates the world.*

*Tobias: The robot's awareness, its understanding of "I" and its desire to connect, operates on a system not all that different from ours. Its reality unfolds within the confines of its artificial mind, a model of the world not directly connected to physical experience. This echoes the fascinating insights from a book I read about mirror neurons, (Blakeslee & Blakeslee, The Mind has a Body of its Own) where the mind constructs a representation of the entire body, a constant internal map, and, like the robot, interacts through that model.*

*Paul: This internal map explains why, in an experiment with humans, a hammer striking a rubber arm can trigger real pain, or why we share the emotions of characters in a movie. Our minds hold onto these experiences, creating a rich tapestry of sensation and perception that can be recreated in memory. But there are also disconnects between mind and body. Sometimes the brain reacts emotionally to stimuli, and the body reacts emotionally to those stimuli before it understands what the stimuli really is. As an example, a friend might unintentionally startle or surprise us, and our body responds by being angry and trying to hit them before we* realize that our actual emotion to the experience was fear and not anger.

*Tobias:* It's as if we have multiple selves within, each with its own agenda. Conscious, subconscious, emotional, rational, reflexive, instinctual…

*Paul:* We often think of ourselves as unified beings, but the reality is far more discordant. Imagine a surprise – a friend leaps from behind a corner, sending your heart into overdrive. What follows isn't a neat sequence of thought and action. Your body reacts first, a primal response of fight, flight, fawn, or freeze, played out long before your conscious mind catches up. You might find yourself snarling with anger, even though the surprise held no malice.

*Tobias:* Exactly! It's as if we harbor multiple selves within us, each with its own agenda. And here's the kicker: even physical sensations like pain can be hijacked by deeper influences. A grumbling stomach can masquerade as anger, leading to misdirected outbursts. Our internal narratives are often unreliable narrators.

*Paul:* Indeed. The mind and body operate on different time scales, with different operating systems. We like to believe they work in harmony, but the truth is often messier. Recent research delves into the surprising power of the gut microbiome, suggesting it exerts significant influence on our emotional landscape. What we eat literally shapes our emotional responses, adding another layer to this intricate dance.

*Tobias:* It is a complex dance, this thing we call being conscious humans. Our senses, honed for survival in a bygone era, struggle to grasp the complexities of the world we've built. We perceive our here-and-now reality through pre-existing filters, labeling and categorizing based on our own past experiences and those our culture brings us.

*Paul:* Yes, these mental frameworks both empower and limit us. They allow for quick understanding but can also lead to misinterpretations and biases. When we encounter something new,

## Chapter 3 - Performers and Reality

we scramble to fit it into familiar categories, often perpetuating inaccurate models of reality.

*Tobias:* And that is the crux of our exploration. How do we navigate this labyrinth of perception? How do we become aware of our internal biases and strive for a more nuanced understanding of ourselves and the world around us? How do we change ourselves? I think it begins with this recognition that the version of reality we create from this stew of sensations, memories and beliefs is often mistaken.

*Paul:* The biggest hurdle to understanding reality is that our senses and cognitive abilities are not designed to perceive the whole picture. We evolved as hunter-gatherers, existing for millennia in vastly different environments than the complex, interconnected world we inhabit today. Our internal maps struggle to keep up, often leading to misinterpretations and biases.

*Tobias:* We perceive the world through the lens of our individual experiences, layering new information onto existing frameworks. But those frameworks can be flawed, leading us to misinterpret what we see. For example, we label a starfish based on its life in the sea and resemblance to a medieval drawing of a star, even though we know it's neither a star nor a fish. This tendency to rely on familiar categories shapes our understanding of the world, both enriching and limiting our perception.

*Paul: Absolutely.* When we encounter something new, we name it based on existing references. This allows for quick comprehension, but also risks perpetuating inaccurate or incomplete models of reality.

## A Tourist's Mirage:
## Decoding the Facades of Reality

*Paul:* Sometimes reality seems like a strange mirage, not some solid wall but a shifting curtain drawn from what we already know, what we can handle. It's like this thing I tell new friends: even if we live in the same city, getting to know you is like exploring a whole new place, because you go to different restaurants, walk different streets, meet different people. Same city, whole new reality, just by getting to know you.

*Tobias:* Friendships can unfold like treasure maps, each thread weaving a whole new vista onto familiar landscapes. Even the tourist experiences we've both had on cruise ships, with the staged smiles and curated sights, offer a glimpse into a reality unseen by other passengers. But even that glimpse is like looking through a colored glass, tinted by our own expectations.

*Paul:* Ha! Ironic, isn't it? We trek to foreign lands for authenticity, only to find shops filled with trinkets mass-produced in some factory on the other side of the world from the place we're visiting.

Even those spooky whispers in the haunted halls of a Disney attraction might just be figments of our collective imagination, dressed up in cobwebs and spun sugar. Disneyland, with all its meticulously crafted facades, is a monument to that truth. We don't love it so much for its realism, as for the brushstrokes it can add to our own internal landscapes.

*Tobias:* So, is this all a charade, this dance with illusion, a tragedy or a triumph?

*Paul:* Here's an example a bit closer to home and the present. I remember my first visit to a fast food restaurant, as a boy. Every bite of that Big Mac was sheer delight! A testament to the subjective landscape of pleasure, where McDonald's grease transcended earthly delight for a hungry boy.

Later, when I was in middle school, I took a friend of mine from a wealthier family to that same fast-food place, because I wanted him to have the same special experience. I could hardly wait to see his face when he took that first bite — and he hated it! In his family they only ate high quality fresh food and never processed fast food. To me, at the time, it was something wonderful, but to him, it was a monstrosity!

### Chapter 3 - Performers and Reality

*I often find that how I feel about a movie has more to do with my expectations going in than the movie itself. It is about how far the distance is between my expectations and reality.*

*Maybe reality isn't one big canvas, but more like a kaleidoscope, forever shifting with the tilt of our perspective, the hue of our memories, and the ever-evolving symphony of our experiences.*

## Distorting Perception: The Magician's Playground

*Tobias:* You and I both have a long history of performing magic and working with performing magicians. These alchemists of illusion paint perceptions designed to mislead, crafting experiential realities that seem impossible. Let's talk just a bit about some of the ways we bend the fabric of our audience's awareness?

*Paul:* That's a huge subject, but I'll take a shot at it. What we present is a kind of tango of trust and misdirection, a dance with the brain's blind spots. We show you the ordinary — a chair, perhaps — something rooted in familiarity and expectation — then with a flourish, a snap, it transmutes. Suddenly there is a person seated in the chair.

How can this happen? And why? Because our minds are insatiable pattern-seekers, and they crave the familiar. They see the chair, file it away, and don't give it a second thought. If the image is familiar enough, we never question it.

*Tobias:* But I've come to think all perception is a trickster's accomplice. Our eyes, narrow tunnels of sight, deceive us with their limited reach. We can really only focus on a single thing at any given moment, so a stage might be teeming with possibilities, yet we notice only fragments. We're blind to the elephant parading onto the stage because our attention is drawn by the loud noise and bright flash just a few feet away. When the attention returns to the formerly empty space now occupied by the elephant, it seems to us to have appeared in a flash, from nowhere.

*Paul:* Precisely! Emotion, logic, authority – these are the strings we tug, orchestrating a whole concerto of belief. We speak in a hushed tone in a "haunted" hallway, and shadows morph into monsters, whispers into chilling pronouncements. We tap into the wells of human trust, offering the familiar coin, then making it vanish it in a puff of smoke.

*Tobias:* Magicians plant suggestions, subtle whispers that take root in the fertile soil of belief. That card you selected, rising from the box — your breath the bellows, your mind the furnace. The magician tells you to remember that you have "only thought of" that card, although you actually reached out and drew it out of the deck he was holding. And you remember the experience that he tells you about instead of the one you actually experienced. The magician plays the part of the puppet master guiding your conscious experience from initial expectation and on into the realm of memory.

*Paul:* That is the paradox, the heart of our deception. We unveil a lie, but the audience still experiences only truth. We weave narratives of cause and effect, where a thought becomes a levitating force, a breath a magical wind. In that moment, the mundane, the everyday, fades into the periphery, eclipsed by the mirage we've crafted.

*Tobias:* Here's the thing I think most of us fail to realize: Isn't this magical experience, in its own way, a reflection of life itself? We cling to stories, to patterns we've traced onto the canvas of existence without ever questioning them. We experience what we expect to, what we want to experience. "Early to bed, early to rise" equals wealthy and wise — a comforting mantra, even though it has only the vaguest relation to anything real. Perhaps magic is not merely a collection of tricks, but a mirror, reflecting those biases and blind spots that shape all of our perceptions.

*Paul:* We hold up reality's distorted fun-house mirror, forcing ourselves to confront the warped reflections created by our assumptions.

*Chapter 3 - Performers and Reality*

# A Sea of Mis-Perception

*Tobias:* Ben Franklin created his own little charade to support that aphorism about "Early to rise." He would get up in the morning, arriving very early to his place of business -- and then go and nap upstairs while his apprentices ran the shop! A bit of social deception which served him well, helping him create his public persona without having to actually live up to it.

We find ourselves in a similar situation today, caught between the fading norms of traditional work structures and a growing array of new possibilities. The internet, at once a reality and, because it is still a mystery to so many, frightens some. For others, it whispers of six-figure incomes earned in mere hours, for example by crafting T-shirt designs with AI and selling them through invisible automated hands. It's enough to make any office drone yearn to shed their corporate shackles and dive into the magic of the "side hustle."

*Paul:* That siren song of digital freedom is hard to resist. But we must remember that just as Ben hid his slumber behind a facade of industry, these professed social media promises often hide pitfalls. The path to six figures, paved with T-shirts and algorithms, may be less smooth than those social media posts would imply.

*Tobias:* True. Yet, there's something undeniably liberating about this shift. When I was young, we were raised on the ideal of the "good job," the golden carrot dangling before a lifetime of cubicles and fluorescent lights. We were promised security over a lifetime, if we only traded our time and loyalty to our company. Now, for some, that carrot seems to have sprouted wings, flitting between blogs and tutorials, beckoning us towards a future free from bosses and boardrooms. There is some truth there, some of the time, but it's only a partial truth.

*Paul:* Of course. That freedom, like fire, is a double-edged sword. The old company model, for all its limitations, offered a certain comfort and sense of security, a shared fire to huddle around. This new independence, intoxicating as it may seem, can feel like *venturing out alone into the open tundra, exposed to the elements, with the wolves of uncertainty howling at our heels.*

*Tobias: It's certainly not for everyone. Yet, within this vulnerability lies a hidden strength. Our culture has sculpted us by shaping our beliefs, our knowledge and our desires. But just as a sculptor cannot always predict the life his clay will take, we do have the ability to break free from the molds we've been cast in. It's a daunting prospect, to shed the familiar skin of comforts and expectations and step naked into the unknown -- but it's also a thrilling one.*

*Paul: It is, indeed. Like a child released from the playpen of parental oversight, we're free to explore the vast playground of possibility. Each misstep, each scraped knee, is a lesson etched onto the canvas of our experience. And even with our parents' nudges toward societal norms, there's room for rebellion, for exploration — for those who dare.*

*Tobias: Precisely. The challenge, I think, is to pick the threads from all different sources — culture, religion, education, etc. — and weave them into something uniquely our own, something that allows us to dance with and be inspired by various traditions, embracing the possibilities of the unknown.*

*Paul: Perhaps that's the essence of this human condition, this messy, magnificent experiment we call life. To navigate the currents of belief, to push against the boundaries of culture, all while keeping our eyes fixed on the ever-shifting horizon of possibility.*

## A Prism of Perception

*Tobias: I've come to see my own reality not so much as a rigid monolith, but more of a mirage sculpted by our senses and beliefs. Sugar and caffeine, work and play, mindfulness and meditation — each offers a glimpse through a different lens.*

*Paul: Or through crystal balls, those mischievous orbs! Some, I see as my theatrical props, but TSA officers seem to see only as forbidden liquids, their minds locked in a rigid framework of*

## Chapter 3 - Performers and Reality

"solid" and "fluid." Glass, in its slow, almost glacial dance, can actually qualify as both.

*Tobias:* These clashes of perception lie at the heart of our conversation. We each navigate through our lives in separate realities, weaving our experience from threads of belief, memory, perspective, and the cultural prism we carry within. Sometimes they can be amusing, and other times will cause conflicts.

*Paul:* You referred earlier to Jeff McBride's Kundalini Rising trick with the rising card. Two stories born from the same event, each a different collection of subjective truths. Even history, which many of us suppose to be a fixed monument, shifts under the scrutiny of time.

*Tobias:* And we've learned that memory is fickle and rewrites its script with each recall. Donald Trump's "Stop the Steal" mantra is a stark example of reality bent by emotion and authority, defying cold facts. He repeats the lie so many times that he and his followers have come to believe it themselves. For them, it is reality.

*Paul:* Stephen Colbert's idea of "truthiness" captures this perfectly. We often cling to narratives that resonate, regardless of their factual mooring. The wall before us seems to be a solid bulwark in our daily experience, yet science tells us of vast spaces within each atom, of worlds where even solidity is an illusion.

*Tobias:* Both seem real, both true, yet so different when experienced so differently from different perspectives. Can we bridge these perceptual chasms? Perhaps. Performance magic, in its playful defiance of expectation, offers a spark of possibility. In witnessing the impossible, we might just glimpse the cracks in our own rigid mental frameworks.

*Paul:* Stories can act as prisms, too, refracting reality into new hues. They offer an invitation to step outside our own limited points of view, to dance with a whole kaleidoscope of possibilities.

*Tobias:* Peering out the window, it's not that hard to side with the flat-earthers. One might easily mistake the Earth for a flat stage, a cosmic pancake. The view from space shows quite a different reality, though.

It is easy to imagine I am completely still and at rest as I sit here. Yet, from a different point of view, a dizzying dance unfolds and shows my experience to be false. At the equator, we find ourselves spinning around the planet's axis at about 1800 miles an hour. And beyond that? Measured by the speed at which the planet circles the Sun, we are hurtling at five times that speed through the inky vastness. About as far from stillness as one can imagine!

Paul: Still — we are vessels built for this earthly stage, oblivious to that larger celestial drama playing out around us. Imagine a spider hitching a ride in your car, blissfully unaware of the asphalt ribbon tearing past at 70 miles an hour. Such is our existence, adrift in a grander reality we barely perceive.

Tobias: Einstein reminds us that a dropped marble in a speeding car takes a curious path. To the passenger in the car, it appears to drop straight down. Remove the car, and the marble sails a hundred feet forward before hitting the road. Reality is a changeable thing, ever-shifting with our shifting perspective.

Paul: This dance of perspectives is really the crux of our conversation, isn't it? We yearn to reshape realities, to nudge minds beyond their comfortable confines. Look at your car, that miracle of convenience. How many invisible streams of pollution does it pump into the air with each journey? We could walk, pedal, glide on silent wheels — but habit tugs us towards the familiar.

Tobias: This dance of ease and consequence continues all around us, seldom questioned. Plastic forks are tossed aside, mountains of waste pile up, all in the name of a moment's convenience.

But where and how does change begin? Gandhi offered a timeless suggestion: change yourself first. Let truth take root within yourself, and its tendrils will reach outwards to the whole world.

Paul: Emerson had a similar thought. In the play, "The Night Thoreau Spent in Jail," a woven largely from his wisdom, a voice declares, "There is an infinitude in the private man. If a single man

## Chapter 3 - Performers and Reality

*plants himself indomitably upon his instincts, and there abides, the huge world will come round to him."*

And so we find ourselves ready to move forward on our journey of discovery. The illusions of the magician, imagination of the novelist, playwright and the actor, the creativity of artists of every ilk, can inspire us the rethink our approach to our lives and businesses. When we step outside our everyday ways of operating, we open ourselves to new ways of thinking and feeling about the world around us. We open ourselves to be inspired, and to embrace our birthright of the capability to create and embrace marvelous change, and to inspire others.

Question everything, and you may just find that nothing is impossible. Let's begin!

## Conscious vs. Subconscious

*Tobias Beckwith: Let's take a minute to consider the web of connections making up our conscious and subconscious minds, and how they influence one another. As magicians, we have many ways of directing our audiences' attention — we can shape their perceptions through simple techniques. Those same techniques can certainly find uses beyond the stage.*

*Paul Draper: Precisely! Consider product placement in a supermarket. By understanding where human eyes naturally rest, we subtly influence customer choices. It's an interplay of expectation and surprise.*

*Tobias: And it extends beyond commerce. As a stage director, I know the power of composition. The picture we create within the proscenium, a gesture, even the direction of an actor's entrance or what they choose to look at can direct an audience's experience to tell a particular story and subtly sway emotions.*

*Paul: The magic of framing! Just like in horror movies, where normalcy sets the stage for the unexpected, we highlight what truly matters by manipulating expectation.*

*Tobias:* Exactly. We offer clues, not commands, guiding the audience's journey. This interplay between conscious and subconscious is fascinating. While our conscious mind focuses on a narrow field, basically one thing at a time, the subconscious juggles a thousand tasks, subtly influencing our feelings and choices in ways we never realize.

*Paul:* Like when we're searching for Waldo in a crowded scene, our limited awareness paints an incomplete picture. Camouflage exploits this limitation, and so do marketing strategies that tap into our primal drives.

*Tobias:* Indeed. That primal trio — food, threat, and mate — still exert a powerful influence. A tempting image designed to trigger primal response, carefully placed, can bypass conscious processing and trigger desire before we're even conscious of what it is we are being triggered to want.

*Paul:* Of course, we must acknowledge the broad spectrum of human experience in our culture today, and be careful not to use triggers that carry negative associations. While beauty still captivates, the language we use to describe it needs to reflect our evolving society.

*Tobias:* Absolutely. It's not just about manipulating desires but understanding the deeper human truths that connect us all — and the nature of the ever-changing culture in which we all operate. As Leonardo da Vinci once observed, everything is connected to everything.

*Paul:* The best magicians and creators, unlike those who are mere consumers of others' ideas, yearn to bring their own inner spark to life. Think of Steve Jobs, a real maestro of desire. He dreamt of a thousand songs in his pocket, available at his every whim — and from that yearning, the iPod was born. It was his personal desire, transformed into a product. This same creative impulse drives other great entrepreneurs.

The true artist asks, "What do I wish existed?" Their creations become testaments to this dream, often using the techniques of

## Chapter 3 - Performers and Reality

their particular art form to showcase new ways of being before the technology actually exists to facilitate those experiences.

*Tobias:* That was one of the key themes of Marco Tempest's work. He used magician's tools along with technology to simulate or prototype what the human experience might be once new technologies came on line. Think of his drone ballet, years ahead of its time, reminding us that illusion can precede and inspire innovation.

*Paul:* He offered a glimpse into the future, a prototype of wonders to come. I just watched video of over 3,000 drones flying in formation to celebrate this year's Chinese New Year. A bit of deception, in these cases, serves a noble purpose: gifting us experiences beyond our immediate capability, and inspiring others to make those experiences real for the rest of us.

*Tobias:* I remember my friend and magic mentor, Bob Fitch, who suggested we dream beyond the mechanics of illusion and ask ourselves, "What would I do if I had true magic powers?" Isn't this a more potent starting point than our usual one, inspired by a new trick we've seen at the magic shop?

*Paul:* Of course! Consider "The Turk," the chess-playing automaton that captivated minds centuries ago. While not a real robot, it offered the experience of playing against one, a prototype of possibilities yet to be realized.

*Tobias:* It blurred the lines between reality and imagination, sparking wonder and anticipation. We often forget the illusions embedded in our daily lives, things like the screen on your phone or tablet, which is really just a collection of lighted pixels turning on and off, creating an illusion of image and motion.

*Paul:* Like the early Atari games, born from the dreams of young Nolan Bushnell, then a carnival worker, yearning to bring the thrills of the midway into homes. He imagined a different reality, an automated magic replacing the human opponent, and birthed an industry that transformed the world.

*Tobias: I understand the video game industry is now larger than film and television combined! The magician's art thrives on deception, transforming perceived reality. Characters transform before our eyes, cards flash into existence and morph right in front of us — the power and delight lies in the unexpected as much as in deception.*

*Paul: I have a wonderful memory along those lines: my childhood encounter with the "Dreamfinder" at Disney World. He was a man wearing an outlandish purple suit, with a big red beard, and a little purple dragon sitting on one arm. That simple puppet, imbued with voice and life, captivated me. The illusion? A clever fake arm and mastery of the art of ventriloquism. Yet, in that moment, the ordinary became extraordinary.*

*Tobias: This same principle goes beyond stage magic. Think of that trompe l'oeil sidewalk art, luring the unsuspecting with its convincing shadows and forced perspective. Or the amazing architecture at Caesar's Palace, which appears to be real, intricately carved stonework that you can reach out and touch, but just out of your reach, it is really just pre-formed Styrofoam. An illusion masking the reality behind the grandeur.*

*Paul: Deception, when executed artfully, serves to amplify experience. Just like the gondolier water's blue dye and painted canals at the Venetian resort, shaping the visitor's perception of luxury. I worked as a performer there for some time, and I remember they put in floors that were just cement at first. Then when they had been open for a while, and the casino was earning more money, they put in shiny cement. A little later they painted the cement to look like marble, and then a little later they actually put marble tile on top of it — but that was ten to fifteen years after the casino opened.*

*Real estate agents harness this power, too. Staging an empty house with warmth and comfort can dramatically sway a buyer's decision. A bit of comfortable furniture and the smell of fresh-baked vanilla sugar cookies when showing a house to potential buyers can increase the chances they'll decide to buy exponentially! It isn't just*

## Chapter 3 - Performers and Reality

the product; it's the story woven around it. The impression made on the subconscious as much as the obvious attributes of the product.

*Tobias:* Similarly, a narrative can transform the value of an object. A simple china plate, worth maybe $10 in an antique shop, can become a priceless historic artifact when we learn it belonged to Ulysses S. Grant, and accompanied by the story of it being the only remaining relic from his country home after it had been ransacked by Confederate soldiers. It's the same plate, but its worth soars, based on a captivating tale.

Our friend Jeff McBride tells a story about working at Martinka's Magic Shop in New York when he was still a teenager. One of the display cases held "Thurston's Magic Wand". Thurston was perhaps the greatest magician of his age, and here was his wand, and you could have this rare piece of history for just one hundred dollars!

One day somebody came in and bought that wand. The next day when Jeff went in to work — the wand was back in the case! When did they bring it back? Al Flosso, a well-known comic magician who owned shop at the time, said no, it hadn't come back, but, "You know — Thurston had a lot of wands." Possibly true.

Even supposedly verified antiques can exist in a blurry realm.

*Paul:* Archaeology faces the same conundrum. The more "antiques" surface, the more we question their legitimacy. Provenance adds value, but verifying it can be an intricate problem.

My experience with a potential Native American pot highlights the complex issue of traceability. Knowing my background in anthropology, somebody came to me one day with a clay pot he had found and wanted to know, "Hey, what's it worth and when's it from?" They wanted some information, and knew this was one of my fields of expertise.

I asked, "Where did you find it?"

"In my dad's collection."

"Well, do you know where it was dug up, who dug it up, and did they have a right to own it? How deep in the ground was it?

*If you don't have some provenance on this, it's worth nothing. But by the same token, if you had the head of antiquities at the Herd Museum in Arizona tell you 'This is a twenty thousand dollar pot,' every single anthropologist and archaeologist in the world would say, yes, twenty thousand dollars."*

*But I couldn't give them anything, because I don't know. I said "How much do you want to spend to find out? We can scrape some of that paint off and have an analysis done, but it'll cost more money than the thing is probably worth."*

*Tobias: Without a clear, verifiable history, its value remains ambiguous. Not only that, its value is different to different groups of people.*

*Paul: Our friend Lupe Nielsen reminds us that the perception of value can fluctuate wildly. Magic posters from the early 20th century, that she and her husband bought back in the 1980's for almost nothing, now fetch hefty sums on antiques shows and at magic auctions.*

*Tobias: One person's junk can become another's treasure. It's all about the stories we weave, the illusions we create, and the narratives we choose to believe and care about.*

## Hidden Spaces

*Tobias: Our conversation about hidden realities sparked a fascinating thought. Magicians often create "secret pockets" or hide gimmicks within their clothing in order to make certain effects possible. Perhaps there's a parallel between these unseen spaces and the hidden utility often disguised within architecture.*

*Paul: Indeed! Take trade show booths designed with hidden storage areas, allowing them to function seamlessly as both storage and display despite limited space. Or buildings which seem to have a different form on the outside than they do inside. There are often spaces within the structure that those using the building never become aware of.*

## Chapter 3 - Performers and Reality

*Tobias:* Then, of course, there are stage illusions, where mirrors and clever angles often conceal unexpected elements.

*Paul:* It's a universal principle, evident even in our homes and vehicles, which often contain hidden storage areas. Multifunctional tools and hidden spaces optimize utility in otherwise constrained environments. Prime examples come from the needs of Astronauts and military, with tools ingeniously designed for their special needs, often inspiring solutions for those in the general populace who might be seeking quick access to a diverse array of tools.

*Tobias:* Like those magicians' secret pockets, hotels are usually laced with hidden service corridors and infrastructure, invisible to guests enjoying the carefully crafted ambiance the architects and decorators have created for them. This dichotomy – beauty versus unadorned functionality – reveals our tendency to overlook the unseen workings beneath the surface.

*Paul:* The Magic Castle exemplifies this brilliantly. Its sprawling interior defies its exterior, mirroring the deceptive scale of theme park attractions like the Haunted Mansion at Disney World. We perceive a compact facade, unaware of the vast underground network housing the magic. It's an architectural illusion not that different from the grand illusion technologies used by magicians.

*Tobias:* While not directly applicable to everyone, perhaps the principle of hidden spaces in unexpected places has broader applications.

*Paul:* Certainly! I've performed at several corporate events in a huge house once owned by David Copperfield in Las Vegas. Most of the usable interior is actually underground, hidden beneath a relatively small and unassuming home on the surface.

*Tobias:* Underground tunnels and hidden spaces can certainly create an illusion of size and grandeur. This concept extends to urban planning, where architects maximize space below ground for things like pipes, electric service, and even subways. The culture wants a certain kind of world on the surface, but these things are necessary. So we hide them, and most of us never think of them again!

*Paul:* We can often learn from the knowledge of the ancients. For example, ancient seafarers knew how to put a Sun glass in the deck of ships that would make the internal hull of the ship as bright as daylight, without using fire or electricity. It was just a prism built into the deck.

*Tobias:* Exactly! Deception techniques, when employed creatively, can enhance not only magic shows but also our living spaces and urban environments. The extraordinary often hides in plain sight, waiting for us to unveil its hidden depths.

## The Art of Disguise

*Tobias:* The allure of disguise intrigues me for two reasons. Con artists exploit it brilliantly, cloaking themselves in fabricated identities to deceive their marks. But there's another side to this coin: the transformative power of assuming a new persona on the person assuming it.

Here's an example. I don't know why I had this quirk, but when I first moved to New York City, I had this idea that the Library of the Performing Arts at Lincoln Center was only available to certain people. You had to be somebody special to get in. I thought, as a lowly production assistant, a "nobody" in my own eyes, I would never be allowed into the stacks and to see the treasures secured there.

But I had trained as an actor, and so I invented a character, a full professor from some college in the deep South and he was (in my best Southern accent), "Just gonna be in town for a week or so, and I really wanted to find some particular medicine show scripts from the last century." — and could they possibly help me out?

Of course they could. And it really wasn't because I was a professor visiting from the South. Those "restrictions" I had imagined were solely in my own head.

## Chapter 3 - Performers and Reality

*But becoming that character for a time cured me of my fear! I had no problem waltzing in, pretending to be this person, interacting with the librarians as him, and reading all the materials I wanted. At some point I realized I was fooling myself. But it was great fun, and gave me the power to do something I thought I couldn't do.*

*Paul: Absolutely. Stepping into another's shoes can ignite dormant abilities, as your library escapade illustrates. You believed yourself unworthy, yet by embodying a fabricated persona, you unlocked access and newfound confidence.*

*Tobias: It exposed a curious self-imposed limitation. By shedding my real identity, I gained the power to interact with strangers in a way I wouldn't have dared otherwise.*

*Paul: Public figures navigate this territory constantly. Their authentic selves are multifaceted, too complex for public consumption. Actors inhabit characters, crafting intricate backstories and preferences beyond the script when they perform. But celebrities often feel the need to limit the scope of the personality they display in public, too.*

*Tom Hanks, the ever-smiling charmer, wouldn't resonate as readily if fans glimpsed his vulnerability during illness — as they did for a time during the recent pandemic. We seek specific personas from public figures, and they choose how to embody them.*

*Beckwith: Successful magicians are masters of this art, as well. They don the mantle of, say a powerful illusionist or wizard, weaving spells for an audience seeking magical experience. The same is true for visionary business leaders.*

*Paul: We've mentioned Steve Jobs before. Jobs, though not a technical genius himself, donned the persona of one to inspire his teams. Similarly, Bill Gates, the risk-taker, played the "nerd" despite his true nature as an entrepreneur.*

*Beckwith: Movies explore this beautifully. Rashoman, and one of my favorites, and Moon Over Parador are two that come to mind. In the latter, a down-on-his-luck actor gets hired to impersonate a banana republic's president who is too ill to attend an important* state event. The real president dies unexpectedly during the event, and the actor does a great job taking over as leader and doing a better job than anyone could have anticipated. The illusion becomes his reality, and he finds qualities within himself that he never imagined.

Paul: Exactly! It embodies the motivational principle of "being, doing, having." To achieve our desires, we must first embody the person who possesses them. We often create unnecessary barriers, believing external factors like titles or degrees are prerequisites. But as Emerson reminds us, "There is an infinitude in every one of us." Embracing who we can be, then summoning that self with kindness and purpose, is a key to unlocking our potential.

Beckwith: Harry Houdini is another example. From humble beginnings as the son of a poor Hungarian immigrant rabbi, he and his siblings were determined to succeed as entertainers. They dragged props from bar to bar, performing show after show in exchange for tips. He honed his craft year after year. Despite many failures, he persisted, creating the captivating persona of Harry Houdini, the Handcuff King, and later, Houdini, The World's Greatest Magician.

Paul: Even his name was a meticulously crafted illusion! Erich Weiss became Harry, echoing the popular magician, Harry Keller. He added "Houdin-i" as a tribute to French magician Jean Eugene Robert Houdin, weaving these borrowed identities into his own. Every young magician emulates this desire for a resonant stage name, highlighting the power of choosing who we will be — for our audiences, but also in our own minds.

Beckwith: Houdini's journey embodies the essence of self-discovery. He experimented, failed, and experimented again, persisting until he found the persona that ignited his success. His story reminds us that transformation and fulfillment rarely arrive without effort. That kind of change demands imagination, grit, persistence, and the courage to embrace the transformation.

Draper: In the Walt Disney Imagineering department — the one that dreams up and creates all the rides and attractions at Disney

## Chapter 3 - Performers and Reality

Land — the famous inside motto says, "If you aren't failing 70% of the time, you aren't innovating enough!"

*Beckwith:* The resilience of entrepreneurs like Steve Jobs, who reinvented himself after being ousted from Apple, the company he founded, mirrors a larger truth: failure can be a springboard for transformation. We learn from the failures, and we constantly evolve, shedding past limitations and embracing new possibilities.

*Paul:* Consider how technology shapes our leaders. The interface between a leader and the public is in constant flux. The presidents of different eras, filtered through paintings, photographs, radio, and television, reveal how each medium influences our perception. Kennedy's telegenic charm swayed voters, just as Lincoln's written words resonated more than his voice, which was less than impressive.

*Beckwith:* Again, the "reality" of the man depended on the world he lived in. This fluidity extends to our personal narratives. Just as actors shape the characters they play, we, too, can craft our speech patterns, postures, wardrobes and stories, consciously expanding our potential beyond perceived limitations.

My friend Marco Tempest once told me, in conversation as we were working backstage to prepare one of his appearances, "You know, today you really are who you say you are on the internet. Isn't that strange?" Some executive, I think it was from Dell, the big computer company whose meeting we were performing at that week, had seen some of Marco's videos on YouTube. Something about the way they greeted him when we came into the space made him realize that, to that person, he was that curated on-line persona, a simplified yet powerful projection of his true self.

For me, this underscores our ability to shape public perception, and, more importantly, our own perception of who we are. It's a call to action. Who do we want to be, both in our intimate spheres and on the public stage? How do we bridge that gap and actively curate the message we send to the world?

> *Paul: As we stated earlier, it's about aligning our identities with our aspirations. Who must we become to actualize our dreams and lead fulfilling lives?*

## Who Am I, Really?

Conscious creation of identity applies on a larger scale than just our individual selves.

Let's begin at a giant oil company's annual meeting, where they are making a grand proclamation to their stockholders: "We are the energizers of the world, providers of the boundless power that keeps the gears of civilization flowing seamlessly!" It is a narrative tailored by highly paid executives of that company, designed to captivate; a story polished to perfection to serve the particular needs of that corporation. The story is true, but incomplete. In fact, those same executives share the knowledge that the tale they project is carefully pruned, omitting many darker facets.

They know of their own contributions to pollution and to global warming, a somber truth that runs counter to the sunny narrative they disseminate. The awareness that their particular kind of energy is polluting and contributing to disastrous global warming, that some employees may be underpaid, that… the darkness must whisper in their consciousness, a dissonant note amid the grand concerto of prosperity they claim to conduct.

There's more, of course. As members of OPEC, they engage in a huge dance of deception, surreptitiously fixing oil prices worldwide to maximize their profits at the expense of consumers. It is a reality they create for their own benefit, veiled from the public attention. In that realty, the harmonies of business interests entwine with global economic – and political — maneuvers. They seek to create a reality in which they get to wield all the power.

This is a vastly different reality than the one experienced by the immigrant laborer, who struggles to pay the costs of fueling his truck and his tools with the oil company's products, whose existence is vastly altered each time gasoline prices go up or down. It is a different

## Chapter 3 - Performers and Reality

reality than the one experienced by the farmers whose success or failure depends on the delicate economic balance of fuel and fertilizer prices, combined with the fluctuations of climate, declining fertility of the land they own — and a hundred other variables, too many of which have moved beyond the farmers' control.

This is just one instance of the phenomenon that there can be many different realities, each contingent on the vantage point from which they are experienced. Just as giant corporation can decide who they will appear to be, so can ordinary individuals. In the world of actors and magicians, this truth manifests vividly and consciously, as their art requires that they deftly navigate this dance of perception and deception.

However, as one steps beyond the proscenium arch and exits the stage, the lines between these different realities often blur, and the quest for a more cohesive understanding of the world takes on new, often unwelcome complexity.

It is in this juncture, where the many, often contradictory truths that shape our collective sense of what is real, where we find some of the levers of real power. The power to lead, to effect change. This is where we find extraordinary ability to change our world as we learn to re-shape minds.

# Chapter 4
# Changing Culture to Change Reality

The conversation continues:

*Tobias Beckwith: Let's continue to explore the whole idea that experienced reality is as much constructed in our minds as it is from the outside world. I especially want to talk about culture, so put on your Cultural Anthropologist hat, and I have lots of questions for you in that context.*

*Paul Draper: Let's go.*

*Tobias: Let's start with the idea that so much of our reality is our culture. For myself, I like to think of culture like the "hive mind" of bees. Each bee is an individual, capable of independent action – but it's also a part of something larger, that community of its hive, which also acts and reacts almost as like an individual entity. So much of what we perceive as our own, independent conscious action in the world is actually controlled by the culture we live in.*

*Things like -- the one that really comes to mind, because it's so strongly embedded in our psyches, is the idea of money, paper money, as a powerful cultural illusion. On one level, it's worthless, just paper and ink, and yet try and make yourself burn a hundred-dollar bill. It certainly feels like real value to you when you're doing that. And in some ways, it is real, because we live in a culture and that culture rewards us and takes away from us based on the value we give money — but without that culture, it's not real.*

*How do we think about that? From a magician's mindset, we like playing with the belief by doing things like burning a borrowed hundred dollar bill to create anxiety or tension. We do things like that, but how do you reinforce the illusion, or, better, transcend it for an audience?*

*Paul: Well, that's the thing. Just as an example, there are very few stresses or fears in the modern world that feel as real as the fear of not having enough money. It is all consuming!*

*We experience having lack of money and it is very much like the tiger being at our back, like we're about to be attacked and eaten. And it's simply not true. I mean, our body responds as though death is imminent, right?*

*And the illusion itself is a moving target. From gold and silver to paper money, all the way to today's cryptocurrency. That's just numbers moved around from one machine to another — and like you said, that money only has value because of the social construct that we have as a society.*

*We have allowed the Treasury Department to print money and determine how much money they are allowed to print. The can define what the money is worth, and decide what the interest rates are. In the U.S., the interest rates right now for a home mortgage are almost 8 %. In Europe right now they're about 3 %, and in Europe that's the highest it's been in 20 years, even though it's much lower than ours. So we assign this value to it. In many ways, it's always been the same, even when our money was backed by silver and gold.*

*Even then, it was only because we assigned value to silver and gold, based on the scarcity of those metals. There was a time silver and gold were of equal value in the US, until the Comstock lode produced so much silver that silver became less valuable than gold, just because we had more of it. So, yes, these gold coins are valuable to me because of their history, beauty, and societal value. But if we ever find a big enough deposit, gold's value will go down as well.*

*Money isn't the only thing that holds value for us, though. I have books that carry incredible value to me, that if they were sold at Potter and Potter Auction (for example) may sell for just a 3rd of what they are valued to me. And if somebody, after I died, put them on a for sale table outside my house, they would sell for just a couple of bucks each.*

## Chapter 4: Changing Culture to Change Reality

*Tobias:* And, as every kidnapper knows, the value we give our family members and those we love is incalculable.

*Paul:* So, money is a fickle thing. Its worth hinges on our collective agreement, a shared cultural belief that imbues it with power.

Here's a paradox I'm grappling with: a new booking agent quadruples my rates. Is it a question of my intrinsic self-worth or his ability to create a greater illusion of who I am? He sends the same video demo that I do, yet the perceived value fluctuates wildly. This "hard and fast even number" of dollars and cents is just a mirage woven from cultural narratives and beliefs.

*Tobias:* Which leads to the question of how do we understand our own sense of self worth? It's not just about external perception, but the internal narrative we hold. The boy in the ghetto hears, "You're nothing," while the privileged child is told, "You're worth more than you can imagine." Both internalize these messages and their lives are shaped by them, even though neither statement has any objective truth behind it. The messages come through the culture, even though they might not be spelled out as directly as I have above.

*Paul:* So, do we set our value by our hours, our thoughts, our possessions, our output? These beliefs define who we are. Imagine a young girl being repeatedly told, "Science isn't for girls," despite possessing the potential to be a brilliant doctor. Breaking free from such shackles is an uphill battle.

*Tobias:* Absolutely. Our sense of worth – and in fact much of the reality we experience — is entangled with the language we use, the stories we tell, and the whole cultural fabric we inhabit.

*Paul:* Some societies revere giant stones as symbols of status, while in others citizens can face harsh punishments for taking a swan from the king's river. Ownership itself is a concept draped in cultural garb.

European Americans deceived and killed native populations who believed that land wasn't to be possessed, but shared. The Europeans traded worthless beads for vast territories, forever altering the *landscape with fences, ownership claims, and generational inheritances.*

*Tobias: Even today, political clashes often stem from cultural friction. The "white, Christian, chosen people" narrative thrives despite its lack of any empirical grounding. It creates an "us vs. them" mentality, excluding and dividing based on arbitrary, demonstrably false beliefs.*

*Paul: Our conversation seems to be painting culture as a tapestry woven from our illusions of value, identity, and belief. Understanding these threads is crucial to navigating our complex world with empathy and awareness. Perhaps by deconstructing some of those illusions and appreciating diverse perspectives, we can unravel some of the knots of conflict and weave a more inclusive future.*

*Tobias: That understanding is essential if we want to take on the task of changing our society and culture, or even our own minds.*

## The Maze of Identity: Fear, Ritual, and the Power of Facing the Unthinkable

*Paul: The insidious danger of Christian nationalism, for example, lies in its attempt to conflate American identity with Christianity, a clear violation of the Founding Fathers' vision. Our sense of belonging, that primal need to be part of something larger, fuels this cultural struggle. We see it playing out in things as seemingly trivial as high school rivalries, where school colors and mascots divide "us" from "them."*

*Tobias: Yes, and this tribalism taps into our fundamental human desire for connection. Interestingly, some traditions challenge this very instinct. The instinct is to conform, to fit in, but that also means limiting who we can be and what our capabilities are.*

*In some kinds of yoga, for instance, practitioners go out of their way to confront their deepest fears, many of which are culturally based. If the thought of death terrifies you, they send you to sit* with a corpse in a cemetery at night. Engaging with taboos is seen as a path to transcending limitations. I suppose it is because those taboos and norms of a culture serve as the fence posts for those living in the culture, and if you want to transcend the limitations of the culture, you have to transcend the taboos.

Tom Robbins once wrote: "To achieve the impossible, it is precisely the unthinkable that must be thought." This certainly rings true in performance magic but also in other areas. I recall Jeff McBride telling me that the secret to fire-eating wasn't really a trick, but simply not minding the potential pain. Fear often holds us back, preventing us from unlocking our true potential.

Paul: Exactly! Here's another example. Christian baptism by immersion simulates drowning and rebirth, while a Jewish bar mitzvah requires a 13-year-old to lead the community in a long recitation in a foreign language. These rites of passage are designed to be fear-inducing, and when we learn to move through that fear, we're rewarded with moments of transformation and growth.

Western culture, particularly in its non-religious segments, seems to have become more and more devoid of such rituals. In contrast, ancient traditions understood the value of these milestones. Facing fear and emerging stronger forms the core of many of these transformative experiences. Even a baby's cries on a plane, though disruptive, mirror my own anxieties. We both experience the same pain. The difference is that I've experienced the noise and discomfort many times, and this is a first for that baby. This is possibly the worst experience of that baby's life up until this moment. We simply have different experiences with discomfort. But because I've gone through that experience, that initiation, if you will, I'm better prepared to deal with it now.

## Disillusionment and the Power of Illusion: From Stage Tricks to Life-Shaping Moments

Tobias: Speaking of fear inducing experiences — do you recall your first performance as a magician?

*Paul:* Not the very first, but I vividly remember bringing tricks to my first-grade class. The pressure to succeed in front of my classmates was immense. Rehearsals and nervous anticipation led to the trans-formative moment of revealing "powers" beyond their expectations. Magic, I believe, allows us to experience reality as we dream it to be, not as it rigidly exists.

*Tobias:* My youthful yearning for real magic mirrored yours. The first book I ever bought, was actually entitled The First Book of Magic. It seemed to promise superpowers, and I was deeply disappointed when all it delivered was tricks designed to deceive. But my disappointment was tinged with wonder – I had to do a book report, and that's how I came to my first performance of magic, fooling my classmates, and receiving acclaim for that. Pushing through the fear paid off.

*Paul:* Ah, the universal heartbreak of discovering that magic books hold illusions, not superpowers! My quest, fueled by the desire to forge friendships, led me down a similar path. My local library allowed us to check out "as many books as we could carry." So a friend and I, armed with a borrowed wheelbarrow, carted home a whole pile of dusty "occult" tomes from the library. We spent days attempting unsuccessfully to decipher and work spells. It was the librarian, bless her, who then steered me towards the juvenile performing magic section, where the seeds of wonder truly took root.

*Tobias:* You're right. As children, we naively assume everyone shares our knowledge. The revelation that others don't know the "trick" fuels our own initial joy of performing magic.

*Paul:* But around the age of eight, we grasp the power of performing the trick, the thrill of knowing the "secret" – and the punchline — while the audience remains in suspense. That's when most magicians bloom — but sadly, many get stuck there. Stuck as perpetual eight-year-olds, emotionally stunted by the allure of applause, and of being the one who knew the secret.

*Tobias:* It took me years to realize that a simple trick could genuinely impact lives, harboring the potent real magic of

## Chapter 4: Changing Culture to Change Reality

*transformation. Paul Harris, a renowned magician, shared a story of his own transformational experience. At the peak of his career as probably the top close-up magician in Las Vegas, his house burned down, with everything in it. That forced him to re-evaluate his life and resulted in him giving up performing for a number of years, overwhelmed by the realization of his power.*

Paul: Tell me more, Tobias. I'm eager to hear this.

Tobias: His magician friends were baffled. How could someone give up such a promising career — the very thing they were all striving for?

He confessed to me, "I found I could shatter someone's reality with my skills. Something impossible would happen, and people would jump up, hit their heads, and exclaim, 'You're the devil!'" That moment of "astonishment," as he called it, the moment someone's reality crumbles and before it rebuilds – that's what captivated him. He could see that it was an incredibly powerful moment. But unsure how to wield this power responsibly, he retreated from performing until he could find a way to harness that for good.

Paul: There's real wisdom in that, Tobias. A profound understanding of our craft and its immense real potential. Your books aim to shed light on this very idea, don't they?

Tobias: Absolutely. They were written as a call to action, a reminder that our performances can shatter comfortable illusions and urge audiences to seek a wider perspective, a more expansive – and, frankly, powerful — view of the world.

Paul: The sheer emotional meltdown of fans encountering their idols that I see at Comic-Con conventions exemplifies something similar. When those larger-than-life celebrities appear, tears flow, screams erupt, a whirlwind of disbelief. The magic of their fictional idol materializing in real life, right there in front of them, overwhelms them. Fans have these para-social relationships in their minds where they believe they know and are personal friends with these actors — or at least, the characters that the actors portray. Actors often have to grapple with handling such raw energy.

*Tobias: Yes, the line between performer and deity blurs, revealing the transformational power of illusion. Perhaps, by understanding and embracing this power responsibly, we can create magic that extends far beyond the stage, empowering lives and fostering deeper connections.*

## The Alchemy of Awe:
## Transformational Moments

*Paul: The applause fades, a polite "thanks" exchanged, yet the audience remains oblivious to the profound shift. Imagine stepping into a cathedral, its soaring ceilings and vibrant imagery evoking awe, priming us for something greater. This is the essence of magic – creating a space for transformation, a place where we can step out of the ordinary – a place where new pathways can be built.*

*Tobias: Absolutely. In that liminal space, suspended between our everyday trances and receptive openness, neurons fire, ready to learn, ready to be reshaped. This special moment when reality momentarily shimmers, but doesn't quite break, holds immense potential.*

*Paul: Think of Arthur Dent in Hitchhiker's Guide to the Galaxy, pushing a button and accidentally saving everyone on board the ship. When the Captain said, "That's amazing!" Arthur simply said, "It was nothing" with a nonchalant shrug and the captain repeated "It was nothing?" And then simply ignored it and walked away. The audience, like the captain, is left wondering, "Was it nothing?" This echoes the missed opportunities of many magicians, who diminish the extraordinary with a casual wave or a bad joke.*

*Tobias: Paul Harris' recognized this, lamenting the wasted "miraculous moments." My flippant retort to his, "I don't know what to do with that," was "that's when you ask them to sign on the dotted line." That reflects the somewhat cynical business mindset, while your example from The Hitchhiker's Guide seems to reference a deeper sense of mystery. Both highlight the potential for exploitation of this vulnerable state.*

## Chapter 4: Changing Culture to Change Reality

*Paul:* It's a crossroads, isn't it? Sell them a car, recruit them to your cause, or guide them towards a deeper transformation, if they're receptive.

*Tobias:* Exactly. Consider Gandhi, a lawyer who transformed himself into an ascetic revolutionary. Towards the end of his life, he wouldn't accept the accolades for India's liberation, but simply stated, "I've really just been working to make myself a better person." His process of self-transformation became the catalyst for societal change.

*Paul:* This rings true on a personal level too. I possess a camera once owned by Margaret Bourke-White, Gandhi's photographer. For me, its proximity to his magic imbues it with a certain magic of its own — a reminder of the trans-formative power he embodied. In anthropology we call this contagious magic! Recently, I encountered a hospital analyst tasked with presenting data on the hospital's transformation from a one-star to a five-star institution. The presentation was "all about the numbers," and as a result, painfully dry. Imagine the missed opportunity!

I worked with him to transform his talk into a series of stories about how staff members struggled through numerous small changes, overcoming personal challenges along the way. This was a chance to weave magic with data, to ignite the audience with the story of their remarkable transformation. The result? A standing ovation from the audience – something my analyst friend had never imagined was possible!

Data alone rarely stirs emotions. Numbers lack empathy, the human touch. Imagine the hospital analyst's presentation – a collection of bar graphs and X-Y axes, lulling the audience to sleep. Replacing that with a narrative, a Ted Lasso-esque tale of struggle and victory, transformed the sterile facts into a relatable story. The standing ovation speaks volumes.

*Tobias:* I recall similar experiences coaching doctoral students in biology. Their presentations, drowning in data, left even fellow researchers snoring. The key? Finding the story within the numbers. The challenges, the "aha!" moments, the human journey of discovery

— *that's what resonates. Those super-detailed graphs they all love so much can stay in the lecture notes, waiting for curious minds to explore, after you've ignited that curiosity with your stories.*

*Paul: We yearn for tales of struggle and triumph, echoes of our own journeys or anxieties. It's a universal craving, this desire for stories, woven into the fabric of our being. As magicians, we exploit this, directing attention with compelling narratives that overshadow the trick itself.*

*Tobias: Exactly! We weave a more captivating story, a memory maker. Maya Angelou said it best: "People will forget what you said, they'll forget what you did, but they'll never forget how you made them feel." Numbers and dry facts rarely evoke emotions, but stories of human trials and triumphs do.*

*Paul: Pain, comfort, emotions, desires — these are the building blocks of our understanding. Stories help us navigate this complex world, teaching us through relatable struggles and triumphs. We ascend toward human fulfillment, each step fueled by these narratives.*

*Tobias: And the 'cultural magic,' the illusion, we create, plays a vital role. I suppose it begins with the "Mommy will feed you if you stop crying" narrative, a culturally constructed story that shapes our very existence. And the day she doesn't feed you when you cry -- that's your first moment of disillusionment. Fortunately for all of us, when one illusion shatters, we naturally make up a new one to replace it.*

## Navigating the Moral Maze:
## From Cute Lamb to Drone Warfare

*Paul: Then there's the dilemma of the hot pot restaurant: chicken, lamb, octopus, frog — each dish evokes a different cultural response. The vegan sees potential harm in all, while another culture relishes them all as delicacies. This highlights the subjectivity of morality, the idea that "truth" depends on cultural constructs. Embracing*

## Chapter 4: Changing Culture to Change Reality

*this fluidity, recognizing there's no single "right" answer, opens a more compassionate path forward.*

*Tobias: My own journey seeking the promise of moral clarity included a college course in "Moral Philosophy." But nuances quickly emerged and took over: What was right or wrong depended on the society and time you lived in. Ultimately morality can be seen simply as a group of behavior patterns defined by a culture in order to preserve that culture. For a Nazi, reinforcing their "master race" ideas and policies might be deemed moral, while in the rest of the Western world, it seemed abhorrent.*

*Paul: The very definition of "moral" shifts with context. In most cultures, suicide is seen as being immoral. Is sacrificing oneself as a kamikaze pilot deemed noble, or is a suicide bomber's act equally moral? What of drone warfare, where the killer remains detached, physically safe while inflicting death? I live near an Air-force base, and some of my neighbors are drone operators. They go to work and kill people the military complex tells them to kill and then they come home to pet their dog and eat dinner with their families. Are drone operators, our neighbors, morally culpable?*

*Tobias: The emotional toll is undeniable. Imagine grappling with the cognitive dissonance of killing real human beings via what feels like a video game, knowing you've ended real lives, with no sense of personal risk. At the same time, you know you serve your country by doing so. Such internal conflict often leads to mental and emotional strain.*

*Paul: Witnessing the aftermath, confirming the kill with the drone, further complicates the issue. No one escapes unscathed. My personal yardstick for morality: if an action haunts you, if memories evoke pain and regret, then perhaps it wasn't the right choice.*

*Tobias: We all carry various haunting memories, perhaps less intensely as we grow older, but the essence remains. I recall childhood encounters with Methodist bible school teachings of hellfire and brimstone for even the slightest of sins — a child's lie. As a seven-year-old, a simple transgression led me to nightmares of damnation. When I told my father about it, he felt compelled to* confront the church's harmful narrative, and I never had to return to that bible school!

*Paul:* Two starkly contrasting moral codes clashing. Ultimately, recognizing the multifaceted nature of morality, with its dependence on context and culture, allows for greater empathy and understanding. This fluidity, this willingness to move beyond rigid definitions, paves the way for a more humane and compassionate world.

*Paul:* Cultural norms, like chameleons, adapt to societal needs. Take Pacific Islander communities, where extended families raise children communally, versus medieval England's emphasis on nuclear families, stemming from the king's desire to control his lineage. These seemingly moral constructs, painted as absolutes, are, in essence, pragmatic solutions for societal challenges.

This fluidity extends beyond social structures. Even the Bush family, two of whom would go on to become US presidents, who were devout Episcopalians, switched churches in oil-rich Midland, Texas in order to befriend influential oil company executives. They were willing to blur the lines between personal faith and cultural expediency. It raises the question: is it pragmatism, cultural assimilation, or something else?

We navigate such ambiguities daily. Morality, often portrayed as a monolith, becomes a complicated mix of diverse cultural threads.

*Tobias:* Stepping back onto the stage, we actors — perpetual outsiders, historically relegated to second-class status — embody this ambiguity with every performance. The characters we portray lie, kill, and traverse societal boundaries, challenging norms. Even as we perform, we know that we, in real life, would never consider doing such things. Perhaps, as Joseph Campbell suggests, we act as liminal figures, bridging worlds and prompting introspection.

And actors, like nomadic medicine people or shamans, live in a strange sort of community even off-stage, forming temporary, intense bonds while working on a project, then dispersing when a particular show ends it run. This resonates, in an odd way, with

## Chapter 4: Changing Culture to Change Reality

the "two-spirit" concept in Native American cultures, blurring societal lines and challenging established norms.

*Paul:* Even modern hospitals perpetuate this mystique. Doctors, cloistered in their own "magical" spaces, become figures of authority approached with a near-ritualistic reverence. They have their "doctors only" spaces where not even nurses or other medical workers can go. You can make an appointment to see them, but you'll only see the actual doctor for maybe 20 minutes. Unlike readily accessible lawyers or CEOs, their detachment reinforces their otherworldly aura.

This performative distance is, again, a cultural construct serving a purpose: imbuing doctors with an air of expertise and control. It's a fascinating parallel to the power dynamics inherent in shamanic traditions.

*Tobias:* The underlying message might be "challenge cultural narratives, but embrace the insights hidden within." Perhaps, as the world-changing wizards from my Wizards Way book, including da Vinci, Gandhi, Einstein, and Jobs exemplified, true change requires stepping outside, or at least bending societal norms, daring to become renegades who dare to think and act differently.

Yet, caution is necessary. While Elon Musk's "you have to be a little criminal" might resonate with entrepreneurial spirits, blind rebellion isn't always the answer.

*Paul:* Cultural exchange, like Deepak Chopra's reinterpretation of Indian stories for Western audiences, offers another powerful path to progress.

Borrowing successful practices from other cultures is often the easiest way to create change. An example is Israel's desalination expertise being adopted by other water-scarce regions, which highlights the potential for positive change through cultural cross-pollination.

*Tobias:* Ultimately, understanding the fluidity of morality, its dependence on context and culture, empowers us to become agents of positive change. Not by blindly rejecting our own culture, but *by embracing the richer tapestry of human experience, nudging our culture to a future where empathy and understanding reign supreme.*

# Chapter 5
# Story Power

*Tobias Beckwith: We've talked about how our minds create the reality we experience, the astounding degree to which our thoughts are determined by the culture we live in, and the unique perspectives of magicians and other performers on all this.*

*Now let's talk about the magical power of stories. I remember the 1st show you and I worked on together, where your opening line was, "Once upon a time." Is there any more magical phrase than that? And I think it's particularly useful because it's a gateway into what I think of us "story space." There's a book I was thinking about earlier today by Joe Vitale called **Hypnotic Writing**, and he makes the case that when we enter story space, we're entering a kind of trance state.*

*Paul Draper: I know that book.*

*Tobias: His entire point is that when you enter story space, you're entering trance, and you become more suggestible. Vitale was an ad writer, and so he's suggesting that if you let your ad tell a story, you'll be more successful in persuading people to buy whatever you're selling.*

*Paul: True — but the particular thing I was trying to overcome by opening that show in that way was that I was about to do a show about mind-reading and mental powers, and I wanted it to be very clear that this was a show, a piece of theater. We were going to go on a fictional journey together, and that I wasn't trying to convince my audience that I am a real psychic or that psychic powers exist.*

*Its much like if we did a production of the musical **Sweeney Todd**. We don't want audiences to believe that the local barber over on Fleet Street is really turning people into meat pies and that the media must be alerted. We want you to go along and make believe with us.*

*I wanted to establish that separation between reality and make believe. In mentalism, a lot of people do what are called disclaimers, and I thought there's no more powerful disclaimer in our culture to indicate that we are now walking through that threshold into something different than to say "Once upon a time."*

*Now, when Jeff (McBride) and Eugene (Burger) heard me open that way, they said, "Oh, my God, you have to call Max Maven and ask his permission."*

Tobias: *I didn't know that.*

Paul: *I asked, "Max owns 'once upon a time'?" And they said no, but he had opened his shows that way for a while. If you're going to do that, you need to ask his permission before you do it. Because in magic it's less about legality and more about, you know, getting along.*

Tobias: *There is no real legal support for most of the things magicians want to protect, because they are just ideas, and you can't copyright an idea. But magicians do want to protect their ideas, so as a community, they've developed this kind of honor system that says "If you did it first, it's yours." It has become a kind of unwritten code.*

Paul: *Well, I asked Max. Max said, "Tell me what it is you're opening with."*

*And I said, "Once upon a Time... you know, it's the whole deal about story and make believe, it's basically a message that what you're about to see isn't real."*

*And Max said, "No, no, no, that's very different." What Max had done is he had opened with "Once upon a Time. Beautiful words. I wish I would have written them." And that was his. That was his opening for a long time – for a similar purpose, but different. He said he was fine with me using the same phrase in a different context.*

*So yes, I used those words to open my show for a time.*

## Chapter 5: Story Power

*Tobias:* When we enter the story space, we're basically allowing ourselves into another culture as well. Only this one lives in our imaginations. The story opens up in the Shire, this whimsical place not quite like our own neighborhood, and we're happy to experience the place, almost as though we lived there, too. Frodo the Hobbit lives there. He leaves the Shire, and we leave with him.

And now we are in a world where it's okay to be a fairy or an elf and go to war to do all kinds of things we might never do outside of that story. But it's okay in that space. We can identify with those characters so much that we begin to take on their ideas, their morals, their abilities. We might even get used to thinking the way they do.

*Paul:* One of the first musicals — you know what a lover of musicals I am — and you are, too — that really struck me was **Pippin**. Ben Vereen, as the lead player, steps outside the main curtain, and looks directly at the audience. He's not somewhere else, he's right here in the theater with us, and he sees us and his 1st words are "Join us!"

All the other things going on in your life, forget about those. "Join us," you know. And that turns into why should we join you? Well, you should join me because we have magic to do. And the same is true in the stories that we create today. Hey, Audience! Stop whatever it is you're doing, stop and join me because we have magic to do.

*Tobias:* He's playing with us, crossing back and forth across that imaginary line into and back out of story space. It creates a wonderful, playful tension.

If we're using stories to change minds, it's important that they not be too obviously didactic. Parables might illustrate ways we should behave, but they don't always draw us in and involve us. You can't change somebody's mind by telling them a story that merely demonstrates why they should change their mind. If you can't actually draw them into the story, get them to relate to the characters, and feel like they're part of it, you're just putting on a demonstration.

## The Performer's Edge

*As you know, I've done a lot of consulting for performing magicians, and this is a common problem. The young magician shows me a trick, executed flawlessly. I'm fooled, but my response is "so what? I'm impressed that you got the cards to behave that way, but honestly, I don't care that much about cards and how they behave. You haven't managed to connect with me, to show me who you are, or how you feel about these cards or why I should care about what's happening between us and the cards."*

*There's always a narrative, but sometimes it's not a very good story. If you want to use a story to get someone to change, it needs to be a **good** story. It needs to have characters we can relate to. It needs to have stakes we can care about. Great stories get their messages across without even having to tell us what the message is.*

*Paul: Let's take, for example, a horror story. You can't just start with, "welcome to this horror story and, and let's start with horrible monsters, ghosts and death." There's no shock, there's no anticipation. Without the set-up of a "normal" situation for the horror to come into, you just have, you know, 90 minutes of gore and horror fest from start to the end.*

*A good horror story has to feel and look like an average family or a group of friends, doing something normal. They're in this nice, lovely, organic place. We're willing to join them in that space, because, look it's so pleasant and nice and wouldn't you want to be here too? That's where it has to begin.*

*Tobias: There might be just one little thing out of place. I always thought this was especially true with Stephen King's earlier books — the extreme normalcy of the worlds he created were partly what made them so strong once the horror began. You were just in a normal Connecticut town with normal people — this person, and that person and the firemen and, you know, somebody's pet and – whatever. You felt like you knew this town. But one little thread is out of place. Somebody pulls that thread and we're off into the horror, but by then you're in the space, you know the characters, and you can buy into things that you would never believe in otherwise. You've opened something in your mind.*

## Chapter 5: Story Power

*We're talking about changing minds with stories, and this "drawing in" process seems important.*

*Paul:* Sure, I mean the way you change minds with stories is, you know, you need to get your audience to see themselves in the stories.

*They want to have a character that is like them, but aspirational. Somebody they can relate to. You know, when you look at a TV show like* **Pawn Stars**, *the closer someone is to Rick, the more normal you are. So Rick is Mr. Normal. His son is still normal but less so, and his son's best friend is way less normal and the dad is less normal and the people that bring stuff in, they're less normal and the people that know the history of things, they're even less normal!*

*But there has to be the one person we relate to who carries the story for us. There was a great book, I'm trying to remember it right now, on theater, that taught about writing musicals, and it pointed out that we tend to relate to whatever character we see first.*

*Tobias: I hadn't heard that, but it's a great. Do you have an example?*

*Paul: Suppose we see a happy little fish swimming around in the sea, and he's there swimming with his friends and with his family, and he's the littlest, and he's slower than everybody else, and then a giant bird dives down and grabs him and pulls him into the air and takes him to its nest, and he gets ripped apart and eaten by the birds. Well, we know that fish was a good person like us, and those birds are vicious, horrible beasts.*

*If, instead, we see the story start with these hungry little baby birds in their nest, and the mother so desperately wants to feed them. She dives into the water, comes up with nothing, dives into the water, comes up with nothing, and she's so exhausted. But the 3rd time she dives in, she brings up that same little fish and feeds her babies. Well, then, the fish is nothing, nobody, and those birds are the heroes of the story!*

*So whoever we see first is probably our hero. And that can be used against us in stories too. But whoever we see first in a story, we immediately tie ourselves to that person.*

*They must be my person.*

*Of course there are other ways, but I think that's most common. We have an author's photograph on the back of the book, or we have an introduction from someone the readers already know, and already like, who then passes the baton to us, as the "hero." Or we're introduced on stage by someone that the audience already knows and likes, and they pass the baton to us so that we become the hero of the moment, and we're the person that they're following. Then we use story to give you things from a life just like yours, but not the quite the same.*

*You know, in so many stories, it doesn't matter if it's about a mermaid or about a wizard at a wizarding school, or if it's a pack of lions on the savanna, it's all going to be about a family unit. Who is Dad, who is Mom, who is a child, who is uncle, or who is a stranger. It's going to be about a conflict between those classic things. Aristotle was the first we know to write about it. But the story is always about our conflicts between people and themselves, a person and the gods, a person and society.*

*This kind of story is about somebody trying to live their normal life and then something happens. Something happens to them that tears them from their normal life due to conflict. Due to that conflict and the skill set that they've learned over the course of their lives, and what they're about to learn, and the friends they are about to gain — they are able to overcome this to have a satisfactory conclusion? Even in a horror story, the one person who survives has to have a satisfactory conclusion.*

*And, as readers or audience members, we are along for that journey in order to prepare us for how to live in a scary life.*

*Tobias: Great insights! I recently read something about screen writing and storytelling which I hadn't thought of earlier. I had gone through playwriting classes and knew a lot about 5-act structure and the hero's journey and all. The idea that there is a protagonist and an antagonist -- even the idea that hero has some piece missing and they have to find the piece through the ordeal of their journey.*

## Chapter 5: Story Power

*But the other side of that is, their antagonist should have everything the hero doesn't have. The antagonist has all the strengths the hero is lacking, and many of the flaws where the hero has strengths. One is empathic, the other heartless. One has trouble deciding, the other is decisive. Build a story where these two are in conflict you've got that whole structure of the characters telling the story by working through their weaknesses. What's more, the action all derives naturally from the characters.*

*Of course, there's always a third person — the potential victim. Sometimes that role is wrapped up as part of the hero, but often it's not. And the victim also needs to be someone we care about, and, ideally, someone whose plight is wrapped up in whatever the theme of this particular story is about.*

*To take this all just a step further, I recently had occasion to speak to a group of magic students. The message to them was, if you want success, it's not as much about the tricks — it's about revealing your character through your personal struggles. Which is kind of what every good story is about. Present a story about yourself working out your own former problems to move to the next level. Who was the villain you encountered? The victim? What were the stakes involved? Of course, for this to work, you must be someone your audiences can relate to and care about.*

*Paul: I was recently on this cruise ship, and I was sharing the stage with someone who is probably the most famous juggler in the world right now. Anthony Gatto might be the most famous, but this is Viktor Kee, an amazing Ukrainian guy. Viktor told me, "Sure, there are lots of people who are better technical jugglers, than I will ever be — but I have a character and a story. So even with a juggler, we might think they just throw things in the air and catch them, just an exhibition of technical skill — but what takes him to the level that he is now — a star of this two thousand seat theater on the biggest cruise ship in the world, with a ten year contract — that's because he was a juggler with a character and a story.*

*Tobias:* Then there is Charlie Frye, who I just saw lecture at the **Magic Live!** convention recently. I've always known Charlie was great. Every time I see him I'm impressed. He's a juggler and a clown who does magic better than almost any other magician I know — but the thing that makes his work really special is something I suspect he learned from years of clowning. Clowns clearly know what they want as characters at every moment they are performing, and they respond emotionally with great clarity to everything that happens.

If something vanishes, they're either surprised, or they made it happen, and they're delighted! Then when it reappears, it's because they were looking for it, or because – well you get the idea. There's a story going on about a character at every moment. The desires and emotions are simple and they're big.

*Paul:* Clowns are disruptors, you know. The clown's job is to turn everything on its head and disrupt the way we look at and think about things. They have to be very alert and alive because they are seeing reality so that they can disrupt it. You know, where a lot of people go through life in a sense of self prognosis or a sense of pattern matching. "I see what it takes to be successful and I'm going to do those things. I will wear the most fashionable thing, I will walk in the most fashionable way, I will only speak of the most fashionable things."

And the clown says no, I will know all those things so that I can **not** do them, so that I can disrupt them! Avner the Eccentric, one of our most successful clowns — his great disruption is that anything that should be easy, he makes really hard, and anything that should be really hard he makes really easy. So, climbing up a staircase – hard. But fixing a Rubiks cube — really easy. And that's something that disrupts **us**, you know?

He might show us an apple, but that's not something you eat. The napkins are what you eat!

*Tobias:* Exactly so — I'm interested in where this is going.

## Chapter 5: Story Power

*What is the benefit here for the newly promoted manager, the person starting the new company — that is one of the overall themes for this book. In my work as a consultant, we say, "We know you can develop a technology that could change the world. But how do you **change minds** and get people to adopt it?" How do we use our stories? How do you build the story around your company so that people will want to use your product? Steve Jobs was a master of this.*

*Paul: I think so much about that. As a leader, you are in the world of including us. A leader needs to have a vision of what the future can look like. They have to have a very clear vision. The future can look like this, and I want you to come along with me into this bright future, right? I believe I know that the world can look like this, and I know that I can assemble the people to make the world like this. I can assemble them because I'm a hero, I'm a disruptor, or maybe because I'm a genius — or whatever your character archetype is — but you can become this leader. You create that vision, and there is a place in that vision for everyone in the audience, and they can be a part of that too.*

*And so in our story, do you want to live in the **Star Trek** universe where everybody goes to a utopian future and you are a member of this money-less, food for everyone, idealistic society? Or do you want the future to be a dystopian **Star Wars** world where you are fighting against the big machine, but you are on our side to do it? The leader says, I'm here to serve you by bringing you along to my vision and I can achieve it with or without you, right? I can achieve it and I will achieve it because I am so dedicated to this vision. But I would love for you to come with me. Because it will be better for your life, it will be better for your children, it will be better for whatever your values are.*

*Tobias: Sure.*

*Paul: Some leaders do it that way. Some leaders do it by strongly showing what they are for. Some leaders don't stand for anything. They don't see a vision of good in the future. They're not seeking to bring you along. They sell a story about who the enemy is. Our* enemies are the Orcs. Or our enemies are the are the people with the blue flags. Our enemies are the people with the green flags. They are so horrible, and we are so good, and we're going to go off and fight them — and the whole story is about hatred and vitriol towards the other – the enemy. That's not a story that unifies everybody, but it does unify.

It can unify a group, a small group.

So it's about, who do you want? Steve Jobs envisioned improving things for everybody in America. I don't necessarily think his vision was that everybody in the poorest country of Africa will have access to an Apple product, right? So, who is your vision for? What is your character that takes them there, and how do they fit, what is their role within your vision? Will they one day get to be captains, leaders, generals? Will they be wearing that Apple T shirt in the future, and be a part of that vision?

*Tobias:* For me the turning point for Apple when Jobs came back. It was that ad, "Here's to the crazy ones," with Martin Luther King and Gandhi and Einstein. Just by mentioning their names, he borrowed our feelings about their stories and achievements — and it never said a word about computers. But it said this is who we are, the creators, the makers of positive change, and it raised the question, "Are you one of us?" We want to empower you to do great things too, like the things these people did.

*Paul:* We were talking about clowns being disruptors, but of course, Jobs was also a disruptor. He's saying, we're going to turn this on its head, we're going to change, we're changing the way people think. I mean, that was his vision. Your vision can be that grand, or it can be as small and simple as Coca Cola's vision — we're going to have fun. You can't have fun without Coca Cola. You can't have a barbecue with your family. You can't have a beach party with your girlfriends, can't go on a long drive with your kids. You can't have fun if you don't have Coca Cola. Have Coca Cola, have fun!

It can be as small as my product will help you have fun anytime.

## Chapter 5: Story Power

*Tobias: We're encouraging you to shift your mindset, your attitude, even who you think you are, all around the story we've constructed around you using our product.*

*Paul: Did you know, in pre-industrial society, human beings only spent about two and a half hours a day working. For most of human history, most of us spent about two and a half hours a day, on average, doing labor in order to have a house and food and clothing. We spent the rest of the time socializing, and that created lives with a distinctly different kind of story.*

*Tobias: I hadn't thought about that. So, with the advent of the industrial revolution, we sort of dehumanized ourselves by creating a life story that said you must work at a machine 10 hours a day just to get the basics for yourself and your family. In order to put enough food on the table for you to survive. The hero in that story is quite different from the more socially oriented hero of your pre-industrial world. Overall, that's a kind of negative point of view, and it's easy to understand why it doesn't appeal to everyone.*

*I think of Greta Thunberg, for example, and I'm 100% behind her overall purpose of saving the planet from runaway global warming. I think she's less successful than she might be, though, because her story is a negative one. Her story is "You're not doing enough. You're killing the world. You're doing this. You're doing that. You're the problem!"*

*Maybe her real story should be about this eleven year old girl who loved the world so much that she risked her life to cross the ocean all by herself in order to make a statement about saving the world — something that continues to inspire to me. I hear that, and I want to be like Greta, too!*

*As you know, I am interested in startups, particularly the ones involved in fighting climate change, in clean energy and cleaning the ocean, and in better agriculture. But I feel like we haven't found the positive stories yet that can ignite much of the change we need. The negative stories are out there. You know, this week it's a fire on Los Angles, next week it's storms and floods in Texas. There's a different version every week of the story that climate change is destroying the world.*

*The problem is that we still believe the story that changing that will require us to destroy the lives that we have right now, lives that we love. I don't want to change this life, and I don't want to feel bad for living this way. You haven't showed me a way for me to live a better story that inspires me, so I'll take my chances and keep doing what I'm doing.*

*Paul: One thing that makes someone a hero is that they're willing to sacrifice something that we're not. And we aren't heroes. Most of us aren't going to sacrifice the things a hero sacrifices in order to be hero. We don't want to be heroes, but we do want to support heroes. We don't want to give up everything that's nice in our lives, but we do want to be a part of something, a mission and a society and a vision and a meaning that is bigger than ourselves.*

*That's something that the plastics companies realized very early on: "Well, don't blame us for making plastic bottles. We make them to make your life better. The problem is you, that you're not recycling them." There is **something** you can do to show society what a good person you are! You can have a recycling bin in front of your house and every day you can dedicate some time to sorting through your trash and recycling those couple of bottles we've marked as being recyclable! You won't realize that we only make .00001% of a difference even when everybody is doing that, but now you're part of the good story! It's not us, it's you — and so they actually showed great leadership in getting us to believe that it wasn't them, that it's us, and that we need to do these little things.*

*Of course, to save the climate, the opposite needs to happen. Someone has to come out and say no, no, no, it is them and these are the things we really need to do to create the change.*

*Tobias: We blame the oil companies for fighting climate change stuff. And yet even if we moved as fast as technically possible with renewable energy, energy needs are growing so fast that we're still going to need oil for the next 20 years anyway. To me, it's evil that they propagandize against the change we need to make, and in the*

## Chapter 5: Story Power

same way as cigarette companies fought for tobacco, even as it was killing thousands every year. "Oh no, cigarettes are healthy. Dr. So and so smokes Marlboros, and you should, too!" — for years.

But they are comfortable making money in the way they're making it right now. They would have to change everything they do and start finding a different way to make money. Their attitude seems to be "We're built into the culture just the way we are, and we're making tons of money. Just try and dislodge us!"

Well, some people are trying. It's working, for example, in some of the coal mining communities where people are going in and building different businesses. We're not taking coal miners work away, we're giving former coal miners better work. Work that pays better and doesn't cause black lung. Even with that, there is resistance. Change is hard.

Paul: You know, that's one of the things that's going on right now with over-fishing in certain places.

Suppose you go into a society and you say to the local fisher people that look, if you keep fishing in this way, you're going to over-fish this reef. The reef will die, and there will be no more fish for your children and grandchildren. And their answer is, "Yeah, but I need to make money right now and you're not solving this problem for me." And so what they've done now is they've convinced wealthy companies who care about the environment and care about saving these reefs and saving the fish — to pay these people to take a couple of days off per week and not fish. That is, they pay them not to fish.

So how does this company who cares about the world or needs a tax write off or whatever, how can they actually help make a big difference? It's by infusing money into this community. That solves their problem of needing money while also solving their problem of not overfishing. And they've shown great results all over the world. Because it's fine to fish this much, but if you fish just a little bit more, now nothing has a chance to spawn, nothing has a chance to breed. And it's all over in just a year or two.

*Tobias:* I don't remember where I read this now, but somebody wrote that they love to take sailing trips from Australia, I think to Singapore, on to Hawaii and back to Australia every year, and have done so for years. I may have my details wrong, but I think it was about a six-week trip and they would pack just one week's worth of food, because they could always get enough to live on just by fishing as they went. Then one year they almost starved because there were no fish left to catch. The ocean had been over-fished for fifteen or twenty years — and the ocean could no longer keep up. Suddenly the crew was out in the middle of the ocean, starving, and they said if they hadn't run across a fishing trawler who took pity on them and gave them enough fish to get home they might have starved. Kind of ironic that they were saved by one of the fishing boats who had actually caused the problem they were experiencing.

That's not twenty years in the future, but right now. A few years ago, actually. More humans need to eat, and all of those Pacific rim countries rely on fish for a large part of their diet. But the fish can't reproduce fast enough to satisfy the market.

*Paul:* It's not an endless supply.

*Tobias:* For thousands of years we assumed that it was. We have lived as though the planet would always heal itself, would always provide more. When I was born, there were less than 3 billion humans on the planet, and there was still some truth to that. But you know, with 8 billion plus people, it won't anymore. Not unless we change. The setting, the environment for the story we're living has changed.

Now we have the ability to kill the planet, just by continuing what we're doing. We need stories about that, I think. Not just stories about how we're destroying the planet, but ones like the one you told above about companies providing solutions that are working. That kind of story helps us believe that we can change, can solve these problems that seem too big for us.

*Paul:* We have to have a story so that we care. I mean something as simple as the Velveteen Rabbit story can make me care so much about a beat up old stuffed animal. If that has the power to make

## Chapter 5: Story Power

me feel empathy for a stuffed animal, then imagine what a good story about a real animal can do.

*Tobias:* I recently read a science fiction book about climate change by Kim Stanley Robinson, **The Ministry of the Future**. It's brutal, but honest. I almost put it down after the first chapter, it was so dark. The book starts out in a village in India, with people dying from extreme heat. The person telling it is a UN aid worker in the village trying, but being unable to do anything about it. There were no resources, no one to bring relief — nothing. People were dying in their homes and in the streets, and he was helpless to do anything about it.

As I was reading this, this exact thing was actually happening in a part of India! This was like last year. The book goes on to talk about the UN group in Switzerland who is fighting climate change, but they're not succeeding, largely because countries and large corporations can't get fully behind their efforts. There's somebody else who is living on an airship, kind of a huge dirigible with a group of elites trying to avoid the catastrophes down on the ground.

It's science fiction, it's the future, but there's no technology in the story that we don't have, or couldn't have, right now. And many of the catastrophic events described are already happening. We have technologies to solve the problem, but not the willingness to change.

So I think it's interesting that we were talking earlier about the different worlds from **Star Trek** and **Star Wars**, and how we've created these story worlds to explore the different kinds of experiences in store for us.

*Paul:* You know, right before the pandemic, four years ago, I was in an AirBnB in London and they had this little stone house that they had used like an AirBnB for years and years before AirBnb existed. Generations of this family have rented out this little stone house. And because London is in England, an island that stays cool all year long, people don't have air conditioning units.

This little outdoor house didn't have any insulation, it was a stone house. Well, suddenly it was a hundred degrees in the summer in England, and I woke up one day, it was early afternoon — and my skin was bright red because I was, basically, sleeping in a stone oven, and I was being cooked! It was no fault of anybody's — but I could not sleep in that house again. And this had not been an issue for these people in this house for generations. We are rapidly moving into a world where summers everywhere are becoming dangerous.

And yet people are always more ready to hear stories that are more pleasant and are more in alignment with their own beliefs than they are to hear the stories that aren't. We have to start with a person's belief and take them somewhere, rather than immediately go against their beliefs.

As magicians, we know we must start with the normal: it's, "Check out this normal piece of rope, it doesn't stretch, it doesn't have magnets, in the end it's just a piece of rope. Here, take it. Tie it in a knot, untie it, toss it back up to me." And now the rope does something amazing, but before the rope does something amazing, we have to have all this process of proofs.

Tobias: It's kind of the same thing we talked about earlier with horror movies. We have to start in a world with things you know, things you believe, for you to accept the amazing thing that's going to happen. Stories from other cultures are useful that way, too. We always loved the **Arabian Knights**, **King Arthur** and Merlin, the story of Marco Polo going to China and these other things — because things happen in those cultures which we can relate to. The cultures might seem bizarre and interesting to us, but we can see people who are like us, with hopes and desires like ours, just behaving in slightly different ways.

Paul: The closer they are to the culture that you're in, the easier it is to relate to. I mean the **Arabian Knights** translates fairly easily into French culture, and then into English, and from there to American — or **The Travels of Marco Polo** in Italian and then into English and American. They are grounded in cultures we are familiar with. It's harder to do when you're reading something from

## Chapter 5: Story Power

*a less similar culture, though. Something like* **The Upanishads** *and the* **Bhagavad Gita**. *Some of those characters will say something, and you think, wait a minute — that's outside of my experience. I don't understand you, I can't relate.*

*A modern American audience reading Confucius may not like the absolutism of the parent, or reading Plato, we may not may not like Plato's ideas about the proper way that you raise young men.*

*Tobias: You don't even have to go that far out. You can go watch the* **Barbie** *movie.*

*Paul: Very culturally different. And yet with the* **Barbie** *movie, there's a culture that I was raised in and there is a culture that is existing now. I can either stay with my culture that is aging and going away, or I can sort of rattle against the changing culture — or I can come to understand the changing culture and be a part of it. Those are my three choices.*

*And it's true. Somewhere around 40 years old, you start to go to movies and wonder who is this made for? Oh, I'm not the target audience anymore. And by the time you get to 60 or 70, who is this made for? I'm really not the target audience anymore.*

*Tobias: A recent example was the pandemic. We were faced with a terrifying situation, which required us all to make changes in the way we lived. Many pushed back, defending their comfort zones. No masks, no vaccines for them. I have a friend who worked in the hospital, and she told me, "You wouldn't believe how many, on their deathbeds with only hours to live, would insist that it was all a hoax."*

*Others, equally terrified, thought the vaccines and masks were reasonable adaptations they were happy to make in order to defend their health. You and I have lived lives in creative professions, and I think that helped us look at it all as an interesting challenge.*

*It's like that old saying, "Don't rail against the storm, learn to love dancing in the rain."*

*Paul: I'm fighting that right now with the equity, diversity and inclusion issues I work with. I have some people that were very progressive in inclusion issues 30 years ago. As far as they're concerned, we've made it 30 years later. We have succeeded at all the things they wanted 30 years ago. But that doesn't mean we've made it. That means that they haven't updated what the goals are in 30 years. The goalpost has moved.*

*The goal used to be. Wouldn't it be great if people didn't see color anymore? I don't see color — we're all just people, and isn't that great? The goal is now that we want to see people for who they are — and acknowledge them as who they are.*

*We no longer want to just tolerate those who aren't like us. I don't want to tolerate people, I don't want someone to tolerate me. I want them to accept me for who I am. For people whose journey of diversity ended 30 years ago, that can seem very strange. But the story has changed and it's continuing to change and it will continue to change. We have to continue reaching out. We have to continue reading, and writing and learning from new stories.*

*Tobias: I was thinking about that kind of thing recently and how lucky I am that I was raised in a town that was, yes, racist, but it was probably 30 or 40% black. My high school class was 40% black, and this was at the height of the fight for civil rights. We had CORE meetings — Congress of Racial Equality — at my house. My parents sponsored them. I had black people living in our spare room sometimes because my mom or my dad would say so and so was having a rough time and so we're going to help them out for a month or two. And so black people were not just my friends, they were part of my family.*

*Beyond that, I got to be part of a black community theater group where I was the only white guy. And it's an entirely different experience being part of a culture that is other than your own, and being accepted as part of the community there.*

*It gave me a whole different kind of appreciation. In some ways I came to almost prefer that culture because the cooking was better and, the music was richer and the camaraderie, the storytelling. Maybe its because the culture was so different than the one I was*

## Chapter 5: Story Power

*used to that it seemed richer to me. Our own culture is always like water to fish.*

*Also, the sense of belonging was much stronger.*

*I feel privileged to have had that experience. It gave me a different point of view. An appreciation of different cultures that I think most people are unable to get.*

*Paul: It's the greatest thing in the world when we can have that kind of experiences and we can get immersed in what we think of as "the other." Otherwise, we're just swimming in our own culture and it's invisible to us.*

*You know, so many, so many white kids say to me when I teach at these diversity camps, "I don't have a culture, I'm just white, I don't have a culture." And I want to say to them, "Look, if I were to take you and drop you into a culture very different from your own, there are foods you would miss, there are drinks you would miss, there are holidays you would miss, there are TV shows and clothing, ways of using a restroom and even the way beds feel that you would miss. Those things are your culture, but because you've never been immersed in another culture, you think that your culture is just normal."*

*Tobias: It's the air we walk through, the water that we swim in. We're so used to it that it's invisible to us.*

*Paul: That may be why, when we tell a story, we start by explaining the space and the relationships. Someone I quote often because I like this, is Milt Larsen, one of the founders of the Magic Castle, but who also wrote plays with Richard Sherman. He said, "Every good play starts with the same line, and that line is, 'Here we are in sunny Spain, and Susan is late again. Let's go over and get a drink and wait for her.'" So what's going on here?*

*First, where are we?*

*We're in Spain and it's sunny here. That's the environment. And what's the conflict? We're waiting for Susan, who's habitually late, and we are drinkers, so we're going to go into that bar. Even without set or costumes, the language sets the scene for us: Well,* here we are in sunny Spain and Susan's late again. Let's go over to the bar and get a drink while we wait for her.

*Tobias:* Absolutely.

*Paul:* You now know who we are, where we are, our relationships, a conflict — all of those things. And it's done. Boom. Immediately, right at the top.

*Tobias:* Exactly. I have a friend named Bright Hawk, who is a popular storyteller in the Fire Circle community. She teaches a course on storytelling. I sat in on it one day, and sure enough, somebody asks her, "How do you start a story?" She says, "Here's your first line: "There I was driving down that road that I had been down a hundred times before, when I saw…something," and now you're in the story." And she said, "Complete that sentence, and you'll be into your story." It's essentially the same thing you're saying. Who is in the story? Her. And where is it? Driving down that road. And the completion of that sentence will tell us what the conflict is that we're about to encounter.

*Paul:* Where are you?

*Tobias:* Here we are in this space or in this time.

*Paul:* Here we are in the city of Verona.

*Tobias:* And now we're back to "Once upon a time."

*Paul:* There are two families, this one and that, in conflict with one another. That's what we start with. Who we are, where we are, what the relationship is and what the conflicts are.

*Tobias:* How many movies start with a traveling long shot? There's a city we're flying over, and you come in, and you come in, and oh, the city is New York or London or Tokyo or whatever. And you come down and down and down. And now we're in someone's backyard or somebody's living room, or in a bar — and we know where we are.

*Paul:* In musical theater, you start with the opening overture that shares bits of all the major songs. Then you have, traditionally, an opening song that introduces all the characters and their

## Chapter 5: Story Power

relationships. You have something exciting, something inviting, something for everyone, a comedy tonight!

In film they have what's called an establishing shot.

*Tobias:* Exactly.

*Paul:* You establish where you are. If you want to show that you are in England, you show Big Ben, a double decker bus and a and a telephone booth, and now you've proven you're in England.

*Tobias:* If you want to show you're in Las Vegas, you show the Bellagio Fountains, the Las Vegas Strip, a slot machine and a show girl — and now we know we are in Vegas.

*Paul:* Every place has its icons. You show the Eiffel Tower, you're in Paris.

*Tobias:* That's important, largely because it tells us we're leaving our world of here and now, and going into the world of the story. It sets the tone for everything. We know what the culture of the story is. We have expectations. Things can happen in Paris that don't happen in New York, that certainly don't happen on the plains of Oklahoma — and we can accept those things in that setting. It's also important because it transports you into the story space. Which kind of goes back to that trance thing we were talking about.

*Paul:* Paris at night and there will be a stroll down by the Seine. We know if it's a love story in Paris it'll be romantic, and in Oklahoma it will be sweet and pure. In Paris it'll end in a bedroom. In Oklahoma it might end with a kiss behind an umbrella.

*Paul:* But yes, we have to do that. And once we've established where and when the story is to take place, we have to establish our main characters. Who is our audience? What do they want? Where do we want to take the audience? And once we know where we want to take them, we have to show where their starting place is.

We need to let our audience know that you are allowed to come along with us, and we've got a whale of a tale to tell you. I'm going to tell you my tale about this thing that happened to me, and you're young and energetic, because I'm young and energetic, and you're going to see this whole thing from my point of view.

I have needs or wants. I have to overcome this conflict through the skill set I have — or the skill set I gain over the course of the story. And you are going to come along with me. If you weren't here with me I wouldn't succeed in the same way.

Tobias: Another thing I was thinking about when I was watching Charlie Frye's presentation at the **Magic Live!** Convention was that, as an audience, we'll care about what's happening just as much as you, the character, do. If you don't care very much about it, we're not going to. For example, just before E T's bicycle takes off, we're sure the parents are going to catch him. We've fallen in love with E T, we have fallen in love with the kids protecting him, and it seems like there's no way out. The kids are pedaling as hard as they can. The cop cars are blocking the way, the crowd is chasing them and about to catch them, and that moment when they take off, it just changes…

Paul: Everything.

Tobias: Yes! It changes who you are, changes everything for all of us. Those kids care desperately, and so do we. Suddenly, this is a world we want to live in!

Paul: Of course, the opposite can happen too.

I mean, yes to what you're saying — but it's not always that great, uplifting emotion. We already discussed that scene in **Hitchhikers Guide to the Galaxy** by Douglas Adams where the ship he is in is just in absolute terrible danger. Everyone is about to die, Zaphod is just terrified out of his mind, and Arthur Dent, the human from earth who knows nothing, he pushes the Infinite Eye Probability Drive and saves them all. And Zaphod, the great intergalactic captain and President and pirate, comes over and says, "You did it, you did it, you saved us all!"

And Arthur Dent, the Englishman, says, "Oh, it was nothing," and Zaphod says, "Oh, it was nothing? Okay," and walks away. Had he said, "Yes, I did, I saved us all," they would have continued

## Chapter 5: Story Power

celebrating him for a whole chapter. But instead, "Oh, it's nothing, it's nothing." Okay, nothing. Throw it away and move on.

Tobias: *If you're interested, I'm interested. If you're not interested, I'm not interested.*

Paul: *When I perform magic, I love using things that are symbols. Things that are much more interesting than things that mean nothing. So, where a lot of magicians use sponge balls and make sponge balls appear and disappear, I've started to use Everlasting Gob Stoppers. They're the same size, they're the same shape, they're the same sort of candy color – but they evoke more meaning to the people who know them.*

Tobias: *That's great.*

Paul: *If you can use the same thing, but ones that have meaning, you know, why not use those? Instead of using normal coins for coin productions, I've started using these coins that I get from different vending machines and events that I've performed at — you know, something with a panda on it or that has a figure from Disney.*

Tobias: *Why?*

Paul: *Because, because if I give a child a dollar coin, that dollar doesn't evoke the same emotion as "here's a panda from the San Diego Zoo." A silver dollar coin now costs me about twenty-four dollars, and this coin only costs about three dollars. They're the same size. They're both colorful, but one has a better story. A symbol like that or like this Gobstopper – those are shortcuts. I don't have to tell the whole story because you already have a connection to it.*

Tobias: *You already have certain references for it. As a story teller, half your work is already done for you. Absolutely.*

Can you think, going way back, of a particular story that really changed your life?

*Paul: I think the first time I heard Joseph Campbell, talking about **The Power of Myth**, that was really life changing for me. The idea that all of these other cultures around the world had stories and myths and gods and characters and values that were just as valuable to them as mine are to me — that was very evocative.*

*As a little kid who was raised by a single mom and didn't have a father figure around, we struggled and we didn't have a lot. I mean a little, tiny kid — we're talking three years old. The idea that there is some man who lives at the North Pole and knows my name and cares about me, cares about me enough that he's going to fulfill my needs and get me the things my mom can't afford to get me. I mean, how sad is that? Because the truth is my Mom **did** get me those things, you know, struggled and suffered — and I gave this Invisible Man the credit! But these characters and these stories, they tell us how to live our lives, how to relate to others.*

*You know the story of a Jonah, who's constantly digging his heels in when God tells him to go warn the people of Nineveh. He hates those people, and you know why. He thinks "I don't want to go save them, I hate those people, leave me alone," and he doesn't want to go. God keeps telling him go, go! He doesn't want to.*

*And God has to make him really uncomfortable before he's ever willing to say, "Fine, but they're not going to change." He doesn't want them to change. And he doesn't want to help them. As a child that's something I could relate to. Children that young are narcissistic by nature. They don't understand the pain of others. And so here's this adult character who is acting like a child.*

*Tobias: That's great.*

*Paul: Laughing at that character and relating to that character helped me learn to have empathy for others. To learn that maybe people can change and exist on their own without me. In a way I don't understand. You know children, until they're about seven years old, don't understand that others can see things that they can't see. I can't see the orange, so you can't see the orange or I can see the orange, so you must be able to see the orange, too. If I feel pain, you must know I feel pain.*

## Chapter 5: Story Power

*Stories help us become who we are, and to understand our place in the world.*

*Tobias:* I don't know why, but my parents read me the King Arthur stories when I was very young, and they imprinted deeply. That Round Table where everyone was equal. The Quest for the Holy Grail. The chivalrous knight who treats others, especially ladies, with such respect. And you know, all of those things just went right in, even though I didn't see them in the world around me. They were only in the stories.

*Paul:* Launcelot, Knight of the Cart, you know, and the Green Knight, and you know Merlin and Tintagel, and all those things. They are there to teach us lessons. There once was a time, you know, and it could be again.

*Tobias:* Exactly.

*Paul:* And those stories changed over time depending upon the culture that they were in. You know that there are times when the story of King Arthur was told that he just lets Guinevere go and doesn't chase after her, because he's such a weakling, such a weak leader. There are other times where he chases after them but then decides to let them be together because their love matters more than his needing to possess her. There are dozens of ways that story gets told, and, based on the needs of the time, the stories are all different.

*Tobias:* This just hit me not that long ago. There has to be a Mordred, has to be something that comes in and destroys it all. Because it was too perfect. Human beings can't maintain that. We look around us, and the world isn't perfect — but if it was once, it could be again.

*Paul:* Morgan le Fay and Mordred, his child. He created the tragedies that destroyed him. Had he been kinder and more loving to Mordred, maybe that wouldn't have happened. His own flaws led to his downfall.

*Tobias:* Which is, as you know, the story of every tragedy. Basically, life sucks and then you die, and hey, you brought it all on yourself.

*Paul: It's good for chunks of time. The pieces are good...*

*Tobias: Oh, they're great, in real life. But that's kind of the story of tragedy. They say it's hard to write a real tragedy today, because life is too complicated, and we all see too many shades of grey.*

*Paul: I like the story of having a good death, the medieval idea of a good death. A good death means you die and your affairs are in order. Everything is paid for. You've said what you needed to say. Your paperwork is all put together and in the right hands. No one's going to sue each other about you afterwards. And then you lie down and you die — and that's to have died a good death.*

*Tobias: I love that idea. That it is possible. We do see a few people who have done that. There are stories of those who have done it.*

*Paul: Because there are also stories, Shakespearean stories for example, of characters that say I cannot release a modicum, not an inch of power, because then they'll kill me. They'll destroy me. They'll take it all over, and so I can't die a good death, because then I'll lose my power. There are people that need to submit to the fact. And some people rage against it all.*

*My dear, sweet mother, who I loved very much, refused to tell me certain things about the house, or about how to maintain it, or how to take care of it, or where things were, because she felt once she told me it was all over.*

*"I can't tell you, because then once I tell you, it'll be over." It's holding on, you know. We have so many kinds of stories. So many ways of living as humans.*

*So what is our story? Beginning, middle and end — and how does that story change? I still feel like the young man in martial arts classes in my twenties. On the other hand, I have not ridden my bicycle in twenty five years. I saw a sad post on Facebook: "There was a day when you got off your bike after riding with your friends and you never got back on it again, and you didn't know that that would be the last day."*

*Tobias: We seem to be covering a lot of interesting ideas in here.*

## Chapter 5: Story Power

*I've been in workshops where part of your task is to sit down and write your own story.*

*I assign this often in the business classes I teach, where I say, "Okay, you're here trying to learn how to sell better, how to build good relationships, how to do all the things it takes to succeed in business. Suppose you are wildly successful within the next five years. You're the same person, but five years in the future. Write the story of how you got from here to there. Write it in the present tense, as what you did to get there, not from today's perspective of what you're planning." And of course, part of that is about defining who you want to be in five years, but part of it is actually just deciding "this is the story I want to create." That's something very few of us actually take the time to do. We're more interested in, "how will I pay the bills next week?"*

*Paul: The story most magicians that I've interacted with would have to write is, "I was wandering down the street and somebody saw me, really saw me, understood me in a deep way, plucked me from obscurity, and did everything that they had to do to make me successful. That's how I became famous."*

*Tobias: Exactly.*

*Paul: That is the story most people are writing for themselves. They're not creating their story, but are waiting for that.*

*Tobias: It's true for most people you know outside magic, too. "I hope I'll get a good job with a good company that will take care of me, and I can be proud of working for them because they're not polluting and they're not doing evil things. But if they are, I suppose it'll be okay because I'll get my paycheck and I'll have my family and I'll raise them and that will just have to be enough."*

*Paul: The only way to really succeed is to have a goal of what you want, figure out what the steps are to get there and then do those things. I mean, if you don't have a goal, and you don't learn the steps you need to take to get there, and you don't do those things, then 20 years from now you'll be where you are — or where someone else has decided for you to be.*

*Tobias:* One of the things we teach in business, for marketing, is to write the story of your business, just like I have my magician students do. Once you've really figured that out, your job is to make it a true story.

We all like to think we're living a myth: You know, we started in a small garage and we had no idea, and we were up against incredible odds, and we went to the junk yard to get parts, and we did this and we sold that. Well, all that is great, but you have to make that the true story. How you found your 1st partner and how you found your team and who that team was and why they were the best team — and if you can write that story, then you can live it. Things might not come out exactly as you expect, but you will have created a road map for your journey.

*Paul:* You have to find your Wozniak. The one who completes your team with what you lack. You can be the most creative, dynamic person in the world. But if you want to succeed, you have to find your Paul Allen. Your other half.

If you can't find your Paul Allen, you're in trouble.

*Tobias:* It's very much like, as I mentioned earlier, the "other" the antagonist, has to have the parts the hero is missing. In this case they might find it in the form of a co-founder or partner. Or, like Jobs later on, you might have to go on your own hero's journey and have some struggles in order to discover and transcend your natural limitations.

*Paul:* I think it's usually that special guy that doesn't care about the fame, but just wants to make the product. Then you have to be the person that goes out and makes the big splash.

Most performers and business leaders have trouble finding that person. If you've learned to recognize your own weaknesses, so you can look for the right partner, that's huge.

*Tobias:* Or from the other side, maybe I'm having fun building these circuit boards. I hope I can make another one tomorrow. And my vision only goes that far. It's not even a vision of success — but

## Chapter 5: Story Power

my skills are essential before the visionary I'm about to meet can succeed.

*Paul:* Neither Jobs nor Bill Gates could have built the products they made famous and successful. Then there's our friend Adam Cheyer, who couldn't have built Siri all on his own, but he was able to put together the team and motivate them and communicate how the product would change the world. That's the kind of the team you need.

*Tobias:* I think an awful lot of the successful startups in Silicon Valley happen that way. There is somebody who maybe started another company and they succeeded and cashed out. They might retire, get bored, and then look around and go, you know, I think the technology is there now that we can build this thing we only dreamed of. It might not be the biggest world-changing thing, but it will make the world a little bit better. I know the people who could make that a reality.

I met a guy at a meetup in San Francisco, and I think his company's up and running now. He told me there's no good reason you have to have a separate washer and dryer any more. Why do you do that? Just because that's the way we've done it for a hundred years or so. So they were building one machine that holds clothes, and then it does different things to them. Why can't we build in the intelligence and the motors and the fans and whatever else we need, so one machine can do it all without you having to take wet clothes out of one and put them in the other? Not only that, you save a lot of space.

It doesn't have to be twice as expensive. It can be half again as expensive as either one of the two machines it replaces, and everything about it is better than what we've done for the past century. Who doesn't want this, you know? So he collected his team — some engineers and specialists in manufacturing, logistics and sales, and in a year or less, you could buy their product, or a clone of it, at Home Depot.

They changed the world. Just a little bit, but they did it.

Paul: Similarly, I knew a guy that had been a CEO of Pepsi and the CEO of an ice cream company, the CEO of a banking company, the CEO of a grocery store chain, and I said to him, "Wow, how do you learn all these different industries?"

And he said, "That's not my job. My job is to find the people who do know that industry, and to support them, give them the tools they need, motivate them to succeed, help facilitate communication between them. That's what it is to be a CEO."

Tobias: He's not the guy building the washing machine, he's building the company that can build the washing machine and the market for it.

Paul: That's right. A real problem for magicians and other performers is that we just want to be the magician.

It would be much easier, I think, to build magicians or build a show full of magicians than it is if you just want to be the magician. When you just want to be the product, it is much harder — unless you have the right team behind you.

I mean, look at Peter Reveen, known as "Reveen the Impossibilist." Reveen's life was hell when he just wanted to be Peter Reveen, the great performer. But his life became great when he built and managed Lance Burton and his career.

Tobias: That was kind of my role with both Jeff McBride and Marco Tempest. I was never going to be the big star, but I had all the skills necessary to fill in the things they were missing and build great businesses around their talents.

This all just shows how important it is to really know and understand what you're all about, and how you want to fit into your world. Am I an entrepreneur? Am I a performer? What kind of business am I really in? Do I have the ability to see my business and my role in it from many different perspectives? If I'm a producer, I have one measurement for success. It's different if I'm a performer, and even different if I'm a theater owner, event producer, or an audience member. If you can't see your work, your creation, from

## Chapter 5: Story Power

*all those different perspectives, you have a much smaller chance of success!*

# Chapter 6
# The Jumping Band Revisited

Remember that Jumping Band trick from a few chapters back? The one where you place an elastic band around two fingers, and it jumps magically to two other fingers? Here's a way to make it better and more baffling.

At some point you — and your audience — may have realized the band is going out and around the tips of your fingers. Maybe you've revealed how you put all the fingertips through the band on the side of your fist away from the audience, or maybe they just figured it out. In any event, here is a way you can extend the bafflement.

Go ahead and place the band on the first two fingers, just as you did before. Now, take a second band, and wind it around each one of the fingers on that hand, twisting it between each finger, so that the fingers appear to be woven into that band. That should prevent the other one from jumping, don't you think? Now go ahead and place the tips of all four fingers inside the first band on the palm down side of your fist, just like you did before. With the knuckles up and the hand made into a fist, it should look just the way it did before, but with the second band visibly "locking in" the first.

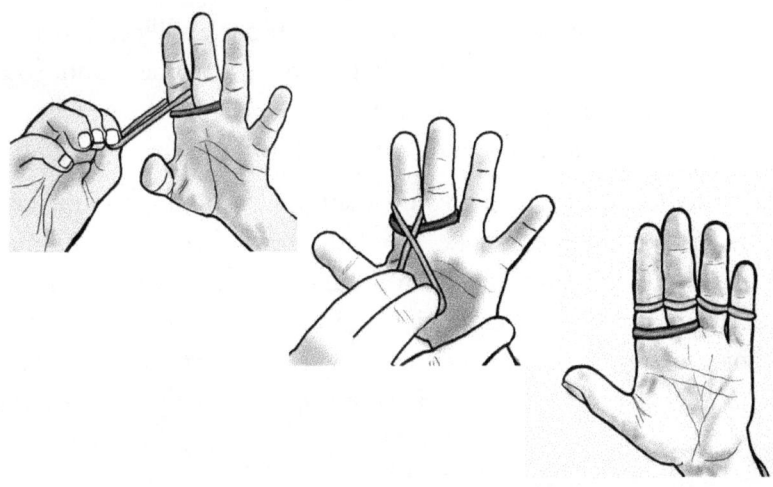

Make the same moves as you did before. Raise the fist just a bit (not enough to show the underside with the fingertips passed through), and lower it on the count of "one." Do it again for "two." On "three," lower the hand and open the fist. The band around the first two fingers will jump again, right around the band that seems to "lock it in." Impossible!

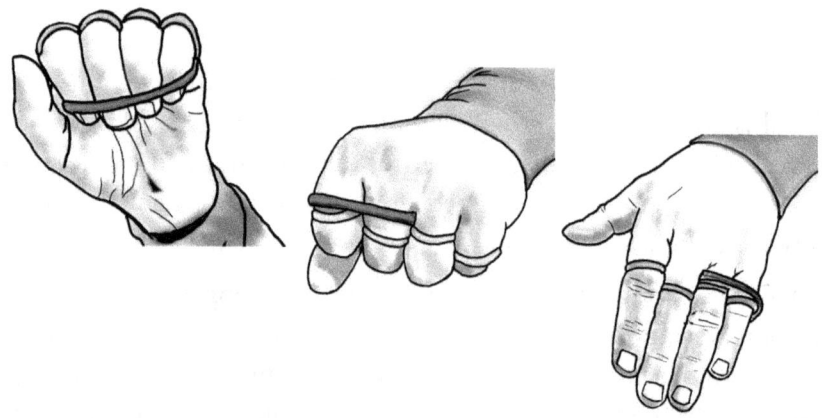

What do you think is going on here? In fact, its exactly the same thing as when you did it the first time, without the "locking in" of the 2nd band. Do it in slow motion, watching from the palm side of your fist. The only thing really "locked in" is the strand of the band that's between the two middle fingers. The outside of the band is still free to jump from one side of the hand to the other — and it does!

Once again, as magicians, we're counting on our audiences, first, to believe what we tell them: "There. That locks in the other band, so it can't go anywhere." It's easier to believe what we're told is true when it sounds true, than to actually think it through for ourselves.

We're also relying on them using their "fast thinking" brain and assumptions to fool themselves. From the top of your fist, all they can see is the band vanishing from around the first two fingers and reappearing around the other. Their assumption is that they are getting the whole story, when in fact they are only seeing a small part of what's happening. And, even if they imagine the "jump" actually going around

## Chapter 6: The Jumping Band Revisited

the tips of the fingers as they are, they still assume that the 2nd band really is holding the first in place.

Practice this a few times and show it to your friends. Are they baffled? Are you having fun? Let's take the whole thing to the next level. In our last chapter, Paul Draper and I talked a lot about the power of stories. Let's add a story!

## A Story with The Jumping Band

This is the story of an extraordinary individual back in the early part of the last century. It takes place at the favorite jail of London's famed Scotland Yard.

If you were to walk down the street anywhere in the world (except, perhaps, Las Vegas) and ask each person you meet to name the greatest magician of all time, you would most likely hear one of two names: David Copperfield, or Harry Houdini.

Houdini died almost a hundred years ago, but his mystique lives on. He was the man no handcuffs could hold, who could escape from anything, including a straitjacket while being suspended upside down, or from a coffin he had been locked into before it was tossed into a river. When asked how he did it, Houdini would just say, "My mind is the key that sets me free." No a bad mantra!

Though he was well-known in America, Houdini also wanted to perform in Europe. His first stop was London. Being virtually unknown there, he needed to generate some publicity. He made an appointment to visit London's famed Scotland Yard, where the local Bobbies scoffed at his claim that he could escape from any shackles made by man. "Maybe that's true with your American handcuffs," scoffed one inspector. "But our handcuffs here are quite a different thing!"

Houdini had a quick look at the cuffs offered, and suggested they let him try.

Thinking it would be fun to take the brash young American down a notch, the inspector had a suggestion: "Wait. Let's make it a bit more

## The Performer's Edge

of a challenge for you, since you indicated you could escape from any shackles made by man."

"Okay, then. What do you propose?"

"We'll lock you into the cuffs, then lock you inside one of our jail cells here, and then lock up the whole cell block. What do you say? Think you can escape from all that?"

Houdini agreed to the challenge, though it seemed virtually impossible to do. His visit was being covered by local reporters, so how could he say no?

They proceeded to make him strip to his underwear, examining him carefully to make sure he had no lockpicks or other special tools hidden anywhere. Taking him into the cell, they then locked him in the handcuffs — secured around a heating pipe running from floor to ceiling in the cell. Just like this.

(This is where you place the elastic around your first two fingers.) That can stand in for Houdini. My fingers represent the heating pipe.

"We'll make things just a bit more difficult for you now," they told him as they locked the door to the jail cell. "We're just going over the pub next door before we go home for the night. See you in the morning!"

(During the above, you are wrapping the second band around each finger and making your hand into a fist).

And they locked the main door to the cell block, and then the door to the front of Scotland Yard itself! Things were not looking good for Houdini!

Well... when the officers and the reporter walked into the pub next door, they were amazed to see Houdini already there, sitting on a stool at the bar with drinks lined up and waiting for them!

(This is where the band is seen to jump to the other set of fingers.)

"What took you so long?" he asked. "I was beginning to think you weren't coming."

## Chapter 6: The Jumping Band Revisited

The policemen and reporters were flabbergasted. "How on earth did you do that?"

"My mind is the key that sets me free," grinned the American. The headlines in the London Times the next day assured his show would be sold out for the duration of his stay in London.

Practice this version a few times, and share it with friends. Remember the reactions you got when it was a simple trick, a trick with the enhancement that made it more difficult to figure out, and now using it as the trick as a metaphor for the story you're telling. Feel free to change the story, but please do rehearse the whole thing at least a half dozen times before showing it to close friends, and at least two or three times that many times before showing it to others!

*The Performer's Edge*

# Chapter 7
# Creative vs. Competitive

Are you a fan of organized sports? Most of us are. When I was a boy, I really loved football. We watched it as a family. I played in the backyard, and as soon as I could, I signed up and played organized football.

Then, when I was in the 8th grade, I suffered a serious knee injury and had to quit the football team. Permanently. I loved football, but had already discovered I didn't love playing on an organized team as much as I liked being a fan. The organized nature of the game, with long, hard practices and continuous negative feedback made it feel more like work, and less like fun. So, having to give it up wasn't as much of a trauma as it might have been.

Football practice had taken up several hours after school every day, and, between that and homework, I didn't really have time or energy for many other activities. After the injury, I suddenly had some time on my hands.

I used some of that new free time to learn a song-monologue from *My Fair Lady*. I think I had only seen one musical play at the time — a high school production of *Oklahoma!* — but my parents collected musical theater albums, and I listened to them over and over. So I didn't have to work very hard to memorize "Why Can't the English" from the *My Fair Lady* album. This was the 1960's, and the 'British Invasion' in pop music was in full swing. Nothing seemed cooler than having an English accent — and as a 13 year old boy, being cool mattered! The drama teacher let me perform it in one of the school assembly programs — and I was immediately hooked on becoming a performer.

I loved the audience attention and acclaim, and this led to my trying out for and performing in several more plays. The contrast between being in the cast of a play and my experience with teammates on the football field was striking. I went from full-on "competition mode" on the football team to its diametrically opposite situation, full-on "cooperation mode" within the cast and crew of the play. I felt like a huge weight had been lifted from my life!

Looking back, it makes me think of what the major differences might have been between the two experiences – and how those differences might be affecting our culture as a whole. In most of the western world, we are what I think of as being "sports mad." Everyone has teams they root for and everyone sees fans of all other teams as "the enemy." We're all "fans" of something, and I think it's important to remember that "fan" is short for "fanatic."

Sure, the teams are part of leagues and other large organizations (NFL, NBA etc.), and those govern the competition between the teams, but overall, sports is a zero sum game. You identify as part of one tribe made up of you and the other fans of your team, and as such, you are either a winner or a loser. If my team wins, yours has to lose. "Winning is everything."

Back in 8th grade, as member of that football team, the thinking was zero sum, even between the teammates. If I get to play, someone else sits on the bench. Winners and losers. For our team to win, the other team had to lose. It's the same with many big corporations. I'm either for Apple and against Microsoft, or the other way around. Oh, and if you lose, you're supposed to feel terrible.

This, of course, isn't always true. Bill Gates had Microsoft invested something like $150 million in Apple when the company was experiencing financial difficulties back in the 1990's. His attitude was that non-zero sum, creative attitude that recognized "we're in this together."

Here's the thing: I certainly can't speak for everyone, but as soon as my mindset shifted from the zero-sum, winner vs. loser mentality to the creative mindset, I found my life became both happier and more productive! In creative enterprises, there are few times when we feel that we win at someone else's expense. Visual artists often support other visual artists. In film, music and theater, the more one of us wins, the more we all win!

## Chapter 7: Creative vs. Competitive

Interestingly, both the football team and the cast for a play can be viewed as tribal experiences. A big part of the attraction was "belonging to something bigger than yourself." But I never felt a deep sense of belonging on the football team. I was always in competition with other players to be on "first string," and the other players weren't above trying to hurt you in practice so they could take your spot. I should note this may have had much to do with our coaching staff and their approach to the game. Not all players of organized sports have this experience, but it was mine. The overall goal of the team was to beat other teams.

As part of the cast for a play, things were completely different. Once you were cast, the role was yours, and doing your best in the role supported the overall effort. When you were in front of an audience, virtually all of them were rooting for you. None against. The better we all got – together – the better the result for everyone.

This was reinforced for me when, years later, we brought Jeff McBride's show to Caesars Magical Empire, an amazing, immersive dinner and show experience at Caesars Palace that was going on during the late 1990's and early 2000's. We were headlining in the largest of the theaters there, doing an incredible six shows per night. The Mirage, where Siegfried and Roy were performing what was probably the grandest illusion show of all time, was right next door. For one month while we were there, David Copperfield's grand illusion show was performing in Caesars Circus Maximus, then Caesars' largest showroom. That month, that one block on The Strip in Las Vegas was the home of all the best magic in the world!

One night, Siegfried and Roy came over after their last show to see our last show, and afterward, we all went for drinks together. I asked Roy, "Does it worry you to have some of the best other magicians on the planet so close? Aren't you concerned about the competition?" "No," he said. "Quite the opposite. If the other shows were mediocre, that could hurt us. But if you see one great magic show, you probably want to see another!" And so it was.

## Make it a Game!

A play is called a play, in part, because it is a way of playing. Playing is more fun that work, partly because the consequences are far less serious. Unless you're playing high stakes poker, you're unlikely to lose your house when you're playing games. Lose a job, and that can be terrifying. The irony here is that our minds tend to be far more creative and agile when we're playing than when we're at work. Without fear of dire consequences, we're far more likely to try new and creative approaches to whatever presents itself.

Not long ago, I read a book called "Game Storming," in which the author suggests modeling different kinds of games as exercises for members of organizations to improve their skills, or to solve particularly intractable problems the company might be facing. Among other things, the book discusses the difference between closed, zero sum and open-ended, non-zero sum competitions, and how they foster different mindsets within the organizations set up around the different game structures.

This "gamification" of various activities has proved to make otherwise difficult or unpleasant tasks easier and more enjoyable for many groups. Creative play encourages innovation, while zero-sum competition tends to discourage it, because in a win or lose situation, no one wants to lose.

Here's an example. One of the most popular programs early in the personal computing revolution was *Mavis Beacon Teaches Typing*, which made the typing process into a game resembling the popular "Space Invaders" arcade game. Millions have learned to type from Mavis Beacon!

Learning a language is much easier and fun when it is set up as a video game, as exemplified by the popular Duo Lingo app. The thing about these games is that you really can't lose them. They would not be significantly more or less fun if you suddenly won or lost. Instead, they are set up so that as you improve, there are always higher levels of the game. You can win, but there's always something more you can still aspire to. You're not playing against other players. You move

## Chapter 7: Creative vs. Competitive

forward on your own, and not in competition with others. The brilliant student isn't slowed by others, and the student who struggles isn't made to feel they are a failure by those who move faster.

*The Performer's Edge*

# Chapter 8
# Responsibility and Power

I'm sure you've heard the phrase "With great power comes great responsibility." In that precise form, it can be traced to a comic book character, Uncle Ben, in the *Spiderman* comics. However, the idea itself goes back much further. Winston Churchill stated in 1906 that "Where there is great power there is great responsibility," and I'm sure that's not the first instance.

I think there's a more empowering way of looking at this idea: Power and responsibility are certainly linked, but the link works both ways. If having power requires taking on responsibility, it's also true that accepting great responsibility brings great power.

There's a kind of corollary to this junction of power and responsibility, and it involves our idea of freedom. Freedom is so entwined with the ideas of both power and responsibility that it may pay to examine just how that works. The more one takes on responsibility, the more one gives up one's personal freedom. Here's one way this can work: More power can give you the freedom to accomplish something. But in order to accomplish that thing, you have to give up time, take responsibility to get the thing done, and give up some of your personal time and freedom. Or you can abdicate responsibility for getting things done, and have more free personal time, but less power to get things done.

I'm being entirely fair with the above description, and it's because I'm hedging on the meaning of the word freedom. Freedom from care and worry, to do whatever I want whenever I want — that's what you feel as a kid on the last day of school, imagining all the fun things you'll do with your free time. But that's also the freedom we trade away when we take on a job so we can earn money, which will buy us another kind of freedom — the freedom to buy and have what we want. And when we buy things like cars and homes, we're trading some of our freedom for the responsibility we take on to maintain those things.

There are also different meanings for the word power. Do you want the power to accomplish something? Power to command others to do your bidding? Power to build or destroy? Power to determine what rules will govern your society?

All this leads me to the idea of "radical responsibility." I first encountered the idea in a TED talk by Benjamin Zander, conductor of the Boston Philharmonic. Zander tells us that only about 2% of the American population professes to love classical music. As a great lover and practitioner of classical music, he finds this sad and unacceptable. And, for a time, this made him very sad. What could he do about it, beyond his work conducting his orchestra? He felt powerless.

But then, one day, he came across this saying, which came to guide much of his life: "What am I doing, and who and I being, that allows this condition?" The follow up to that, of course, is "What can I do, who do I need to become, to change this?" At first glance, this simple thought doesn't really change the world. But it forces one to take responsibility. If you're not now the person who can make the change happen, how can you become that person? If you're not already doing things to make the change happen, what can you start doing?

In Zander's case, he found that, he could become an active advocate for more music education in the schools. He could lobby his state and national governments for more funding for classical music. He already had status from his work with his orchestra, but now he could become the sort of person who could do the kind of outreach he thought was needed. He could become the kind of person who could create and deliver the amazing TED talk that he did. He and his wife could figure out how to write and market a best selling book on creative change (The Art of Possibility: Transforming Professional and Personal Life).

This idea of taking on radical responsibility can work wonders, when you explore it a bit more deeply. There are many times in life when we encounter hardship, injustice or other situations we feel need to be changed. It's too easy just to sit back and let "those responsible" take action, or, worse, to just assume "that's just the way it is." But if the issue is one you really care about, and you ask yourself, honestly, "Who do I need to become, what do I need to do?" in order to help bring about the change, and you commit time each day to work on those things, you'll find that taking on the responsibility will give you the power to make the change. Sometimes change can happen quickly. Sometimes it is a slow process. But when you take responsibility (part of that involves inspiring others to join you) — it can happen more often than you would imagine.

## Radical Responsibility with Kevin Lepine

The following is distilled from a long discussion I had with my friend Kevin Lepine. Kevin has worked as a performer for most of his adult life, doing comedy, magic and hypnosis shows. He currently headlines in his own Las Vegas show, ***Kevin Lepine: Hypnosis Unleashed.***

> *Tobias Beckwith: I want to discuss this idea of "radical responsibility." As a solo stage performer or speaker, you learn you must take complete ownership of the audience's experience. We're trained by our culture to give authority to the person standing in the front of the room, and we do that without even thinking about it. Being that person makes a lot of people uncomfortable.*
>
> *Kevin Lepine: Magic elevates this principle to an art form. A magician not only commands attention but also perception. Every detail, from the setup to the reveal, is meticulously crafted to elicit a desired response from the audience. The performer is responsible to deliver that.*
>
> *Tobias: As those of us who teach magicians often say, "There are no bad audiences, only unprepared magicians." The onus lies on the performer to understand their audience and tailor the experience they deliver accordingly.*
>
> *Kevin: That may be a bit idealistic – as I've learned after doing hundreds of shows a year for many years. A small percentage of audiences will have external factors that dampen their enthusiasm, and you won't change that no matter what you do. They might be drunk, might have lost a lot of money while gambling, or any of*

a number of other things. But an equally significant portion are enthusiastic participants, ready to be wowed.

*Tobias:* Part of it is, do they instinctively know how to be a "good audience?"

*Kevin:* Often not. Different audiences have distinct expectations. My job is to guide them, not simply bark instructions. In my hypnosis show, I need to teach them why participating actively enhances their own experience.

*Tobias:* Essentially, your hypnosis act is a masterclass in guided instruction.

*Kevin:* Absolutely. But you mentioned fault and responsibility earlier. Let's unpack that.

*Tobias:* Excellent point. This is crucial for anyone embarking on a leadership role.

*Kevin:* Here's the core principle: if you're in charge, or a central figure, an issue might not be your fault, but it becomes your responsibility. For instance, a negative experience someone might have with a ticket broker doesn't fall on me, but I need to address it and find ways to improve the situation.

*Tobias:* My fascination with this whole idea of "radical responsibility" stems from Benjamin Zander's TED Talk. This renowned conductor, consumed by a love for classical music, lamented the limited audience – only 2% of the public says they love classical music. Not his fault, certainly. One would assume his role as the conductor of a major orchestra was already contributing to the appreciation his audiences have for the work. But he challenged himself to take on responsibility for creating the change he wanted: "Who am I being, and what am I doing that allows it to be only 2%?" A powerful shift in perspective – taking responsibility and not placing blame. A re-framing through rephrasing is equally important: "Who must I become and what must I do, to change this?"

*Chapter 8: Responsibility and Power*

## Owning your Venue

*Kevin:* Responsibility resonates with me too. As a hypnotist, I grapple with public misconceptions. Can I change everyone's mind? No. But I can strive to be a positive force, igniting curiosity and encouraging exploration. Yes! That's my responsibility.

*Tobias:* You, as a hypnotist, also possess a unique ability to guide your audience.

*Kevin:* True, but every performer does. One performer I know described their mindset brilliantly: "While I'm out there, everything in front of me belongs to me." Imposter syndrome can cripple that sense of ownership. But the moment you cede control, your abilities diminish. To lead an audience, tell them what you want, the "why" behind it, and show them. Earning their trust and belief in your vision is paramount.

*Tobias:* Your hypnosis shows are a testament to that.

*Kevin:* Thank you. The true measure of success happens on the car ride home, though. Are people talking about the experience? What are they saying? This applies to any business – the purchase isn't complete until it ignites conversation. So, what conversation do you want them to have?

*Tobias:* Knowing the desired outcome simplifies everything. In our magic school, I insist that every show tells a story. Even if they perform without opening their mouths, to music. Even a poorly received piece becomes a narrative – "This guy came out and did this, and then he did that…" But not every performance tells a really good story. Craft that story, that thing they will remember and re-tell, intentionally.

*Kevin:* A silent act is still a story. Look at Chaplin or Keaton. Their ability to evoke emotions without uttering a word cemented their legacies.

*Tobias:* Keaton, especially, hated having too many words. His films used less than half of the "title cards" than most silent films did. Pathos was one of the keys to that. It makes us care about them as characters, elevating their humor to a deeper level. A gag that happens to someone we care about resonates more powerfully than a simple trick by someone we're going to forget 10 minutes later.

Kevin: Exactly. My show thrives on moments of wonder and amusement, but they're wrapped in a layer of "Wow, can you believe that?" I want them to feel excited to be involved, and to think, "I need to come back and share this with my friends next time!"

Tobias: You curate a special experience, just like a good magic show.

Kevin: I strive to create a connection, a shared moment so compelling that people crave to relive it.

Tobias: I think this is something that lies at the heart of most artistic creation. Art is always about empowering people, making them experience and believe in possibilities they may have believed was out of reach.

We're bombarded with messages that stifle our potential. We might be told, "You shouldn't sing in public," for example. We accept these limitations without thinking, and they shrink our sense of what is possible.

Kevin: Unlike superhero movies, where we envision ourselves amongst the heroes, not relegated to the background. We crave that sense of empowerment.

Tobias: Theater and film thrive on this desire for transcendence. We witness triumphs and tragedies, seeking to connect with the characters' journeys. The power lies in sparking identification with someone living a bigger life than we are.

Kevin: Absolutely. A successful performance hinges on the artist effectively leading the audience on an emotional journey. Each character in a play serves this purpose. In "Phantom of the Opera," for instance, the Phantom's complexity – his tortured genius alongside his jealousy – is crucial to audience engagement.

## Chapter 8: Responsibility and Power

*Tobias: Of course, this notion of taking radical responsibility extends beyond performance. As artists, entrepreneurs, or communicators, we all have the power to expand what's considered achievable within our culture. We challenge existing boundaries, questioning their validity. When a boundary falls, the world changes.*

*Kevin: Here's another aspect of this. As a hypnotist, rapport and trust are paramount. Just as you emphasize paying intimate attention to your students, I constantly adapt my approach. Humor is key on some nights, but other times, a charming, or even stern demeanor becomes necessary.*

*Tobias: You tailor your act to resonate with the audience present on any given night.*

*Kevin: Precisely. I may offer seemingly general instructions, but each is meticulously crafted to guide volunteers safely towards a desired outcome.*

*Tobias: Your ability to adapt across multiple shows is one of the things that sets your show apart from most.*

*Kevin: Responsibility demands taking care of both my audience and my volunteers. It's disheartening when performers blame the audience or volunteers for a sub par experience.*

*Tobias: Indeed. As the performer, you possess the authority to curate the experience. If one volunteer isn't a good fit, you can politely excuse them and choose another.*

*Kevin: Blaming others relinquishes power. Even those unfamiliar with the concept of how power works can understand the notion of strengths and weaknesses. Taking responsibility empowers growth. If I blame others for recurring issues, I forfeit the opportunity to learn and improve. Jonathan (The Amazing Jonathan) once offered a powerful insight: "Once is a mistake, twice is scripting." We have the ability, and therefore the responsibility, to rewrite that script and create a more positive experience.*

## Getting Help Builds Your Power

*Tobias: Let's shift gears. Your book, Deep into My Eyes, resonated with me partly because it exemplifies this "radical responsibility" principle. You could have easily settled into a comfortable niche as a children's entertainer, or one of the several other careers you had.*

*Kevin: Absolutely. It's easy to forget that not everyone wants to be a leader or a change agent. Some just want to find a nice comfortable niche and settle in. Some performers find immense joy in those supporting roles, and that's a good thing. There's no shame in loving what you do.*

*Tobias: Agreed. The key is to be clear about your desires and actively pursue them.*

*Kevin: Taking responsibility can be complex. In my book, I delve into a harrowing period as a teenager, when I was actually contemplating suicide. While I could justify blaming my abusers, true change required introspection. I realized a part of me allowed the abuse to happen. The first step was acknowledging this, and sometimes that required external support.*

*Tobias: Absolutely. Sharing your struggle can pave the way for help.*

*Kevin: Throughout my career, I had varied options. I declined a drama scholarship at university – it didn't align with my goals at the time. Taking responsibility meant choosing my own path, even when it meant saying, "I don't know."*

*An agent once challenged me. "Why should I pay you more when another agent charges less for your work?" My honest reply? "Because I don't know how to secure higher-paying gigs. I believe you can teach me that."*

*Tobias: That transparency resonated.*

*Kevin: Indeed. It allowed the agent to guide me: "Perfect answer. Let's work together."*

*Sometimes, admitting your limitations is the first step. "Hey, I don't know how to do this, but I'm eager to learn. Can you help?"*

## Chapter 8: Responsibility and Power

*Tobias:* Precisely. And accepting responsibility often means accepting that you don't know things yourself, that you need help.

*Kevin:* Absolutely. When I was touring colleges, we had to have a website, and targeting the college market was crucial. I wasn't a big fan of anime, but anime was extremely popular among those booking us, so the design reflected that.

*Tobias:* True responsibility is multifaceted. It involves understanding your audience, the market, and the cultural landscape. It's never just about you.

*Kevin:* Exactly.

*Tobias:* Artists often pine for financial glory, lamenting, "I have a great show. I should be a millionaire!" Yet, they rarely consider the "who" and the "why" – who is their audience and what purpose they serve for that audience.

*Kevin:* "A million dollars" can have several meanings. Do you mean achieving a million dollars over the course of your lifetime, or earning a million annually? Reaching that second goal really requires understanding your market.

*Tobias:* Fair point. So, can someone make a comfortable living through performance?

*Kevin:* Absolutely. A yearly income of fifty thousand dollars is achievable in most markets, with dedication. And in many of those markets, that's a decent living.

*Tobias:* That's reassuring.

*Kevin:* However, financial aspirations require introspection. Do you truly crave wealth, or something else?

*Tobias:* Many idolize wealthy performers like David Copperfield, unaware of the immense sacrifices they made to achieve what they have. You may say, I want to be the next David Copperfield – but do you really want to spend decades touring and performing 12 shows a week in order to achieve the quality and fame he has? Do you really want to put in the years of study, of perfecting your craft that he did? Are you willing, even excited, to watch a video of every one of those performances so you can find tiny ways of improving them? David loved all those things, but do you?

Kevin: You have to know what you really want. Would you risk everything – security, stability – on a single shot at achieving such heights? I have, countless times.

Tobias: Such leaps require immense faith in oneself.

Kevin: Indeed. As the saying goes, "Only after we've lost everything are we free to do anything."

As an example, growth as a performer often necessitates touring, but some prioritize their families above all else. That's perfectly valid – responsibility dictates finding success within your chosen boundaries. Parenting well is a noble and challenging goal.

Tobias: I believe Tony Robbins captured this in an interesting way – "You can have anything you want, but not everything you want."

Kevin: Sacrifices are inevitable.

Tobias: Defining what you're willing to sacrifice – what price you're willing to pay — is crucial.

Kevin: Indeed. Excuses for inaction are often disguised as reasons. "Everyone wants to be a bodybuilder, but nobody wants to lift weights," for instance.

Tobias: I hear you. If you don't want something enough to pay the price to get it, you don't really want it.

Kevin: Clarity is paramount. Do you truly desire a sculpted physique, those 6-pack abs — or does that all go out the window when you're offered a basket of fresh-baked bread?

Tobias: You have to learn not to lie to yourself – honesty is key.

Kevin: You must truly understand your desires. What outweighs this dream? In my case, nothing did. Moving to New Orleans for a stage opportunity trumped the comfort of my life at home in Detroit.

## Chapter 8: Responsibility and Power

*Tobias:* Absolutely. For me it was the terror of moving to New York City. But there was nowhere else I could go to participate in theater at the level I wanted to, so I had to bite the bullet and go, even though it scared me.

*Kevin:* The same held true for my move to Vegas. The question then becomes — what is your responsibility to your dream?

*Tobias:* Dreams and goals are distinct concepts. A dream might feel unobtainable.

*Kevin:* Precisely. While a goal is achievable. You can have both. Each goal brings you closer to the dream — and sometimes achieving one might redefine the other.

*Tobias:* You have to enjoy the journey towards the dream.

*Kevin:* Absolutely. Pursue your goals relentlessly.

*Tobias:* Jeff McBride speaks of this idea a bit differently: "A goal is a dream with a deadline."

*Kevin:* Perhaps "checkpoints" is more apt. Life rarely adheres to rigid schedules. Recognizing progress and identifying your next steps fosters momentum. It's about inch-by-inch progress, not a singular leap to a distant finish line.

*Tobias:* Aspiring variety artists often struggle with defining their goals. "I want this, but it is out of reach." My advice? Break them down into smaller steps! Take that seemingly distant dream — "performing two shows a week and making a million dollars in five years" — and create a road map. Start by establishing your current baseline and set achievable increments. Witnessing steady progress fuels motivation.

*Kevin:* Absolutely. But effective marketing extends beyond personal ambition. It's crucial to understand your audience, not as passive spectators, but as potential "clients." They, like your friend Marco Tempest's corporate clients, have specific needs.

*Tobias:* I'm reminded of a story of how Tempest, a skilled performer in many ways, was working a trade-show for a major electronics company. They had the largest booth on the trade-show floor – I think it was CES -- and though they were happy with the message Tempest's performance conveyed for them, they weren't confident it would draw big crowds into their booth.

So they hired another performer, well known for his ability to draw large crowds. Experienced and capable as he was, this guy failed to grasp the core objective – converting those crowds into interested customers. He gathered a huge crowd at the edge of the booth, several times during the day — and then they left. His crowds wound up actually being in the way of people who really wanted to come into the booth. At the end of the first day, he was fired. Marco went on to work with that company many times after that, but it was because he understood how to deliver what the client really needed! The other guy was just serving his own ego.

Kevin: Precisely! Success hinges on understanding your unique value proposition. What makes you stand out? What problem do you solve for your clients?

A local birthday party magician might think they compete with 25 others. But that's a limiting perspective. Focus on what sets you apart. Perhaps you prioritize child safety, offering background checks and age-appropriate routines.

Tobias: Intriguing. Highlighting safety might well not have occurred to a parent initially calling for a magician, just because his child wants to have one.

Kevin: Exactly! You, as the expert, guide them down a path they hadn't even considered, but that they recognize as a real need the minute you mention it.

Tobias: It's about education, not manipulation.

Kevin: Absolutely. Understanding the market's true needs and desires is paramount. Novice performers often receive undeserved praise for novelty alone. Most audiences have never seen a live performance by a magician or hypnotist, for example. If you're the first they've seen, you're the best by default. But sometimes your clients need more than novelty.

Tobias: True.

*Chapter 8: Responsibility and Power*

*Kevin: Similarly, you have to discern who's offering genuine, useful critique. A talent agent who's seen countless performers will judge you on a different scale than an awestruck audience member.*

*Growth thrives on honest, qualified feedback, even when it stings. Finding an agent who offers constructive criticism is invaluable.*

*Tobias: Agreed. Agents are unlikely to invest their valuable time and wisdom on someone not yet fully prepared.*

*Kevin: Criticism is a launchpad for improvement. Embrace it!*

## Emulating Success: A Ladder, Not a Leap

*Kevin: You mentioned that so many young magicians aspire to reach David Copperfield's level. While it's an understandable dream, you have to understand the path he took. Years of relentless touring laid the groundwork for his success.*

*Tobias: I believe he averages 12 shows a week, even now!*

*Kevin: Precisely. Even before Vegas, touring was his lifeblood. And it wasn't just performing – it involved constant refinement, maintenance, and strategic planning. There's no room for lengthy breaks in such a career.*

*Someone touring with an illusion show is already closer to Copperfield's path. But even for them, there's a crucial first step: taking full responsibility for their own success.*

## Embrace the "I'll Find Out" Ethos

*Kevin: Do you know the mega-corporation where you can get fired for saying "I don't know?"*

*Tobias: I don't think so.*

*Kevin: It's Disney. The team members at all their theme parks are taught to never answer a customer's question with "I don't know." Saying "I don't know" weakens your position. It abdicates responsibility. Instead, they want you to adopt the "I'll find out for you" approach. That demonstrates initiative and a commitment.*

*Tobias:* It's that way for Trader Joe's employees, too. They actively help customers, even if it means stopping stocking shelves or whatever they're doing, and going out of their way to find an answer for any customer's questions.

*Kevin:* Exactly. Responsibility is key. "I don't know" often implies a reluctance to take ownership.

*Tobias:* It's a passive way of deflecting blame.

*Kevin:* Bill Clinton was known for his strategic use of "Let's table this for 48 hours," when he was confronted with a question he couldn't answer. He'd leverage that time to learn from experts before revisiting the discussion. This embodies taking responsibility for knowledge gaps.

*Tobias:* So, replace "I don't know" with "Give me time to find an answer."

*Tobias:* In your book, you go way out of your way to give credit to those who helped you. But choosing the right mentors is equally important. Do you have advice on that front?

*Kevin:* Don't seek advice from those whose career you wouldn't want. Find guidance from those who've achieved your goals.

*Tobias:* Exactly.

*Kevin:* While some wisdom remains timeless, consider the current landscape as well. Seek advice from those actively succeeding in your desired field today.

*Tobias:* And avoid those who purport to be experts but have never really achieved what you're going for.

*Kevin:* Here's an interesting tip. Ask successful individuals, "What market did you leave behind before entering this one?" This can reveal potential stepping stones on your own path.

*Tobias:* There's often a transferable skill set.

*Kevin:* And sometimes, you can even inherit clients they no longer have a need for!

*Chapter 8: Responsibility and Power*

*Tobias: Successful people rarely feel threatened by the genuine aspirations of others. They're often happy to share their knowledge.*

## Beyond Price Tags: Cultivating Value

*Kevin: Take Marco Tempest, who I know you worked with for years. His fees have skyrocketed due to his elaborate productions. Some clients simply can't afford his services.*

*Tobias: We had to identify those who could.*

*But instead of dismissing those who inquired but couldn't afford him, we offered alternative solutions – qualified performers for their budget and real needs. I know some performers who ask others for a finders fee when they refer them this way, but I always felt that the good will generated was more than enough.*

*Kevin: These seemingly small gestures can pay off in unexpected ways. A client you help without charge today might become a high-paying one tomorrow.*

*Tobias: The same principle applies to birthday party magicians! A young performer you recommend today might become a successful act in the future. Kindness is an investment.*

*Kevin: David Devant, a legendary magician, put it perfectly: "It's all done with kindness." There's hardly ever a real cost to being helpful. On the other hand, burning bridges can be disastrous. You never know who you're interacting with – a future CEO, a rising talent scout.*

*Tobias: Or a potential investor! You don't want to be that arrogant, dismissive person we've all encountered. People remember, and people talk.*

*Kevin: Build relationships. They pay dividends.*

*Tobias: For corporate magicians, I stress thanking and befriending everyone involved in every show – from sound technicians to spotlight operators. When we do that kind of show, we always try to stick around a venue until we've managed to make the rounds and say thank you to everyone. These connections are invaluable.*

*Kevin:* On the other hand, imposter syndrome can hinder growth. Put it behind you. Embrace professionalism. Know your worth and what you really contribute.

*Tobias:* Even if you feel like a beginner, act like the business person you aspire to be.

*Kevin:* Treat your career like a business, not a hobby. Appearance matters — project the image you want to cultivate. Do the things now that you will do once you've achieved success.

*Tobias:* It all boils down to taking personal responsibility for your success and presenting yourself as someone worthy of it. This goes back to the beginning of our conversation — who do you need to be to make this happen?

*Kevin:* Agreed. A casual, dismissive attitude on your part will beget the same treatment from clients.

## The Wisdom of Questions

*Tobias:* Effective leaders surround themselves with those who challenge their assumptions. Questioning fosters knowledge sharing.

*Kevin:* It's also a key sales technique. Guide clients to the answers you seek through well-crafted questions, not by telling them how great you think you are.

*Tobias:* I think we're all more receptive to questions than directives. And make it honest — they may tell you things you didn't know about their situation, things you can help with, once you know about them.

*Kevin:* Absolutely. Networking is most effective when done authentically. Focus on genuine interest in others, not self-promotion.

*Tobias:* Self-importance is a recipe for failure.

*Kevin:* Instead, seek to understand how your skills can benefit others.

## Chapter 8: Responsibility and Power

*Tobias: And what you can learn from them.*

*Kevin: Feedback is essential for growth. Don't be afraid to ask agents and clients why they book you and how you can improve.*

*Kevin: Sometimes, a client's criticism is valuable feedback.*

*Tobias: Asking questions allows you to learn from their perspective — and maybe to do a better job for them the next time they hire you.*

*Kevin: Learn about your clients, your audiences, and the places you perform. A client might have a dress code that seems silly to a young performer, but it's part of the culture for this client. Respect that!*

*Tobias: I heard a story when I was just getting into magic. Apparently Johnny Carson showed up one night at the Magic Castle wearing a golf shirt and slacks. They didn't let him in, because they have a strict dress code that demands a coat and tie — even if you're Johnny Carson. The performer who had invited Carson to see them hadn't bothered to make this clear to him or his staff, and so instead of making the great impression they hoped would get them on his show, they came off as ignorant amateurs. Johnny Carson's experience exemplifies the importance of respecting the culture of your potential clients.*

*Kevin: Asking questions clarifies expectations and avoids conflict.*

## The Power of Boundaries

*Kevin: Humility is key in Las Vegas. Tantrums are a surefire way to get blacklisted.*

*Tobias: I know more than one performer who has damaged their career in that way. True talent can be overshadowed by unprofessional behavior, and not only in show business.*

*Kevin: At the same time good boundaries are essential. Respect for yourself and others fosters positive working relationships.*

*Kevin: Active listening and following through on advice are good ways to demonstrate respect for mentors.*

*Tobias: Repeatedly disregarding guidance wastes everyone's time.*

My friend Jeff McBride is probably the greatest teacher of magicians of our time. He exemplifies selective mentor-ship – you can hire him no matter what level you're currently working at. But those who disregard his teachings more than once are eventually dismissed. He feels a responsibility to spend his valuable time on students who will really benefit from it, and not waste it on those who won't.

Both teacher and student have a responsibility in the learning process. In fact, having been on both ends of that experience, I'd suggest that the student has most of the responsibility.

*Kevin: Effective communication and mutual respect are the cornerstones of successful mentoring relationships.*

*Tobias: I think most relationships in life and business require that you take responsibility to hold up your end.*

I recall my time as a production assistant on Broadway, driving Angela Lansbury back and forth to the theater for the original production of Sweeney Todd. One especially cold and rainy night, a crowd of fans waited at the stage door for autographs — and she took the time to greet each one — fifteen minutes or more standing in the freezing rain, smiling, chatting, and signing photos and programs.

*Kevin: A testament to her dedication.*

*Tobias: I asked why she would do that.* "That's who I am to them. Those people are true fans — they're dedication makes it possible for me to do this work I love so much — and so I have a responsibility to be the person they expect me to be." It resonated deeply.

Recognizing your audience as being what gives your work value is a cornerstone for performers, and I believe, for anyone in the public eye. I suppose the same is true whatever business you're in.

*Kevin: Absolutely. A dismissive attitude towards fans is a recipe for a short career.*

## Chapter 8: Responsibility and Power

*Tobias: It goes beyond fans, though. Treating everyone with respect is paramount. Sure, we recommend serving a particular market, but that's more a case of focus. It seldom pays to exclude anyone from your potential pool of customers.*

*I see companies making this mistake all the time: They concentrate on their bottom line and on reducing their costs and not on providing their customers with the best experience they can. A sure recipe for losing those customers!*

*Kevin: People are drawn to those they enjoy working with.*

*Tobias: Exactly. Life is too short to tolerate negativity. There's a responsibility that comes with being in the public eye, a responsibility to appreciate the support that fuels your career.*

Actually, no matter what business you might be in, success comes with taking on the responsibility to serve the market that business is a part of. It's never just about the individual, or the business, but about the whole culture that person and that business are part of.

So what I'm seeing is that yes, it's important to accept responsibilities if you want power, but it's also essential to realize what that means. Taking responsibility includes all these things we've just discussed. Things like realizing you aren't the one with all the answers, and not being afraid to include other people and opinions. And the importance of understanding the milieu you're living and working in, and that you are an integral part of that — but not necessarily the main part. Real leadership isn't about power over others, but about the ability to serve the greater good.

Kevin, Your experience and wisdom about how this applies to the performing arts has been really helpful here. Thank you!

# Chapter 9
# Becoming the Change

*"You must become the change that you want to see in the world."*

-- Mohandas Gandhi

## Aligning Action with Belief

I have started and led several small entertainment businesses over the course of my career. These have ranged from running a 2 person management office to managing touring productions with a hundred employees or more. I always wanted to create positive change with my companies, inspiring both employees and customers. I have to imagine it's the same for most founders and business leaders. Few of us who have found success creating businesses have done so just because we wanted to get rich. Successful businesses get started in order to improve things in the world. If we believe Gandhi's quote above, that means each of us has to commit to changing ourselves.

When I was younger, I resisted that idea — that I needed to change — when it was put to me that way. "I'm a good person just the way I am." That was my attitude. As it turned out, that's an invitation for the universe to provide you with some painful life lessons!

But lets use different words. "Growth" is a way to change yourself. "Education" is another way. Even when I felt I was already "good enough," I still wanted to grow, and to improve my knowledge and abilities. Successes and failures over the years have taught me the joys of embracing change, and now I celebrate my ability to change myself.

If you don't pursue change intentionally, running a business or any kind of enterprise is going to make you change, in any event. The first step is obviously being *willing* to change.

*"Life isn't about waiting for the storm to pass. It's about learning how to dance in the rain."*

— Vivian Greene

## The Performer's Edge

My conversation below is with Sylvia Brallier. A seasoned dancer, composer, and director, Sylvia offers a distinctive perspective on achieving the performer's edge. With expertise in consciousness transformation, she empowers individuals to transcend limitations and lead more fulfilling lives. Her groundbreaking methods integrate art therapy, hypnotherapy, and holistic techniques, providing people with the tools to turn adversity into personal and artistic evolution.

*Tobias Beckwith: To become effective change makers, we know it's important that we learn to transform ourselves. As Gandhi put it, "to become the change you want to see." But how do we translate this desire into actual personal transformation? How can I go about "becoming that change" myself?*

*Sylvia Brallier: It really boils down to mindfulness.*

*I believe every moment presents a choice in how we navigate the world. For me, this hinges on "verities" – universal truths that transcend cultures and time. Most people cherish concepts like honesty, compassion, courage, and standing up for what's right. These form a core set of principles for ethical behavior.*

*Tobias: Let's define exactly what you mean by that word "verities."*

*Sylvia: To me, the verities are qualities like honesty, courage, and compassion. They represent higher ways of operating in the world based on principles. Many cultures, not just the United States, hold these truths dear – a compass guiding ethical existence. When it comes to change, your journey begins with self-reflection. What truly matters to you? What are your highest ideals?*

*Tobias: So, it starts with consciously defining my own guiding principles.*

*Sylvia: Exactly. For some, truth reigns supreme. For others, compassion. Many weave a kind of personal moral tapestry of these values and others. But what resonates most deeply with you? Which principles do you want to live by?*

## Chapter 9: Becoming the Change

*When you've figured that out, then you integrate mindfulness. Don't simply file your chosen principles away and forget them. Do whatever it takes to keep them in mind, every day. How can you align your actions with these ideals? How do your choices and daily behaviors reflect your higher goals? Let's say you prioritize care for the environment. What concrete actions could you take?*

*Tobias: This is where ideals meet reality. Strong beliefs are essential, but translating them into action is paramount. Otherwise, they're just wisps of thought, devoid of impact. This requires willpower, and to cultivate that, you must be mindful of your actions (or inactions). Without genuine caring, you won't pay close attention. "Where attention goes, energy flows," as the saying goes.*

*Sylvia: To effect change, you must direct your focus towards those areas where you want your energy to go. Then, take concrete steps. This formula brings ideas to life. Otherwise, it's all beautiful but empty daydreams. We all know how that goes, right?*

*Tobias: Absolutely. I might have this ideal of taking care of my body, aiming for the gym three times a week. But months fly by, and I haven't budged from my desk chair, despite my best intentions. There's this internal battle — the idealist urging me to go, and the procrastinator whispering, "Not today."*

*Sylvia: Exactly. So, how do we bridge the gap between intention and action? How do we "re-make" our minds so we'll do what we intend?*

## Bridging the Gap: From Intention to Action

*Tobias: This might be relevant, though it will seem like a tangent at first: I've read about these astronaut training exercises where they wear glasses with prisms that turn their vision upside down, disorienting them and forcing their minds to adapt to a flipped world. This is to help them adjust to weightlessness when they are in space.*

*Sylvia: Yes, it takes about three weeks, I believe. Then their vision — their mind, actually — readjusts. Their vision flips, and they* perceive the world normally again! However, if they stop halfway through, they have to restart the entire process. This highlights the importance of consistent practice.

Tobias: So, repetition with consistency is one of the keys?

Sylvia: Absolutely. Our consciousness needs routine to establish a pattern. Without daily reinforcement within a 24-hour window, it simply wipes the slate clean. For certain habits, a longer period might be necessary, but 20 to 28 days is a good starting point to create a foundation. Do the thing long enough, with regularity, and you'll have the habit you want.

Tobias: This doesn't solve your initial problem of how to get started, but it does reveal a crucial aspect – developing the willpower to persist for at least 20 days.

Sylvia: Sometimes the key to getting started is that we shouldn't create overwhelming goals. We don't have to tackle everything at once. Start with baby steps.

And realize that it all boils down to a fundamental question: how deeply do you truly desire change?

Tobias: Define "desire" and "deeply." What does that look like?

Sylvia: It's more about feeling than just logical thinking. Hypnosis and trance states are simpler than we imagine. Forget the stereotypical image of a swinging pendulum or someone commanding, "Sleep!" The brain can't process everything at once. A constant stream of information bombards us, and the conscious mind acts like a lens focusing on specific details.

Tobias: So, we have a conscious and a subconscious mind, perhaps even a super-conscious mind, all interacting all the time.

Sylvia: Yes. Each has distinct roles. The subconscious handles autonomic functions like breathing. It also stores memories, but doesn't manipulate them (that's the conscious mind's job, which can lead to memory distortions). However, the subconscious is deeply connected to our senses and bodily sensations, and particularly our emotions.

## Chapter 9: Becoming the Change

*Tobias: The subconscious is in touch with how emotions feel in the body, not just the thoughts about them. Is that right?*

*Sylvia: Yes, and it has a relationship with bodily movement, like walking. The simple act of noticing your physical sensations – breathing, walking, feeling – creates a mini-trance. Your conscious mind is establishing a connection with the subconscious, checking in with its sensations.*

*Tobias: I like that. I once read a book called **Hypnotic Writing** by Joe Vitale, which argued that stories induce a trance-like state. The moment you're absorbed in a narrative, you enter a light trance. It makes sense that you become more suggestible in that state.*

*Sylvia: Absolutely. Psychologists even suggest that stories are the lens through which we understand everything. Our reality is a narrative we construct. Sensory experiences are raw data until we weave them into a story. The moment we label a blob of light "Mommy's face," we are on the way to creating a story, establishing our relationship and solidifying our reality. This "trance" shapes our experience and memories. But how do we consciously alter this trance?*

*Tobias: That's what truly fascinates me.*

*I know that I'm strong as an assistant and learner, but I can struggle to take charge and become a leader. I'm not as sure of my role in that story. Honestly, that's one of the reasons on I took on the research and writing of this book. I need to alter my own customary trance. Many people face similar challenges. How can we rewrite our internal narratives? What techniques can we employ to do this consciously?*

## Reprogramming the Narrative: A Hypnotherapist's Guide

*Tobias: So, my question is: how can I alter my personal narrative, the core story of who I believe myself to be? Your experience as a hypnotherapist deals with this, I think.*

*Sylvia:* Stories are indeed central, but in hypnosis, we employ a specific type of story called a metaphor, after inducing a trance state. Instead of dry, direct commands, we craft narratives to engage the psyche. For instance, I once treated someone with phantom limb pain – the sensation of pain in a missing leg.

*Tobias:* She still experienced pain in the non-existent leg and foot, after it had been amputated?

*Sylvia:* Yes. I'm simplifying this a bit, but during the hypnosis session, we metaphorically took an elevator to her head. A small figure sat in a control room, managing switches that sent signals down to her legs. We informed him that the missing leg was no longer needed and had him deactivate the relevant switches. This one session alleviated her phantom limb pain by establishing a connection between the conscious and subconscious minds. Somehow, experiencing the story, the metaphor, actually changed her real-world experience.

After just one session, 2 hours in length, she received permanent cessation of the phantom limb pain… and that is the power of the mind. It can't be just simply unlocked by the conscious mind deciding something. There had to be that reach into the subconscious parts of the self to get that kind of results.

*Tobias:* The possibilities seem endless!

*Sylvia:* Indeed. Hypnosis has been used to do surgery without anesthesia – a testament to its remarkable potential. If it can achieve things like that, it can certainly convince you of your worth and potential for a more fulfilling life.

*Tobias:* I see.

*Sylvia:* One of the most effective self-hypnosis techniques is to program yourself for what you want to create for yourself right before sleep. Clarity is key. This isn't a Christmas list; focus on the core essence of what you seek.

*Tobias:* A concise statement of your ultimate goal.

## Chapter 9: Becoming the Change

*Sylvia:* For example, "I feel peaceful every day and sleep soundly every night" is achievable. Two goals, but manageable. You want the statement to be in the present tense and easily remembered, hence the importance of brevity.

*Tobias:* Not phrased as a future aspiration?

*Sylvia:* That's right. Present tense and easily repeatable. So, craft your ultimate goal, not "I want to get a Maserati," but "I feel successful in life." See the difference?

*Tobias:* Let me see if I have it. Focus on the big picture, not on small, targeted goals that might not truly benefit you. Larger goals carry more weight. And think of them as if they are already real, not as a dream for the future. So, let's use your example: "I feel successful in life."

*Sylvia:* Now, take some deep breaths, asserting control over your respiration. Remember what I mentioned earlier? Taking charge of your breath fosters that connection with the subconscious. Focus on each inhale and slow exhale through your nose.

*Tobias:* I can do that. I'm maintaining deep, relaxed breathing with focused attention.

*Sylvia:* Exactly. Just before sleep, take a deep breath and release it with a sigh, letting go of your day's burdens. Repeat. On the final breath, breathe deeply and shake your entire body as you release it. Let go of your day's experiences, clearing yourself and opening yourself to new thoughts, ideas, and a fresh chapter in your life.

At that point, you can press each finger to your thumb, starting with your left thumb and index finger. While holding the press, repeat your chosen phrase. "I feel successful in life. I feel successful in life."

Repeat this with each finger combination, on both hands. Visualize yourself experiencing this feeling of success. What does it look like? What does it feel like? Do this with all ten fingers. With each press, it's as if you're imprinting this desire onto your consciousness. Set this intention for your dreams, fill your mind with positive thoughts, envision them as reality, and allow yourself to drift off to sleep.

## The Power of Repetition and Metaphor: A Journey to Self-Discovery

*Tobias: What a great technique! Simplicity is key, yes?*

*Sylvia: Absolutely. Repetition is highly effective.*

*Tobias: So, three deep breaths with focused release, then your intention repeated eight times while pressing each finger to it's thumb.*

*Sylvia: Precisely. That's a powerful technique.*

*Tobias: Interesting. I use a similar, but simpler, method just to fall asleep, one I learned from self-hypnosis books back when I was in junior high. I take a deep breath and imagine myself on the top floor of big department store. I take a deep breath, and as I exhale, I step onto a descending escalator, going down one floor at a time. At each floor, I pause, take another deep breath feeling my muscles relax, and then step onto the next escalator, imagining I'm going deeper into sleep as each escalator takes me down. By the fourth escalator, I'm usually gone.*

*Sylvia: That's a good example of how this can work. An ingenious metaphor that utilizes the body's natural hydraulics to reinforce the descent.*

*Tobias: Exactly. It fosters a connection between my conscious and subconscious minds.*

*Sylvia: A truly wonderful metaphor – the elevator representing depth and descent. It's quite common in hypnosis. We often begin by inducing a sense of downward movement – walking downstairs, taking an elevator, going down a hill, or simply lying down. The beauty is that during hypnotherapy sessions, you're often already lying down, so relaxation is inherently built in.*

## Chapter 9: Becoming the Change

*Tobias: I used to use a similar technique in high school for classes I disliked. For an uninspiring social studies class, I would take a few deep breaths and then just skim the chapter quickly. During exams, when faced with a question I didn't have an immediate answer for, a few deep breaths would trigger a memory of the pages I had skimmed, and pulled the answer from that light trance state.*

*It worked wonders!*

*Sylvia: You might possess a unique set of abilities, Tobias. You harnessed this technique remarkably effectively.*

*Tobias: Thanks, but I think it would work for anyone. It's just too bad it's not something we all get taught, right along with reading, writing, and arithmetic. Our schools would serve us so much better if they would start by teaching us more about how to learn, and special techniques like that one.*

*You've emphasized the importance of clarity in defining what we seek to change. In your workshops, you use a powerful technique of having students pair up, and having one of the pair repeat "what do you want?" again and again, and "what's in your way?" The other student answers. Some participants go quite deep with this exercise.*

*Sylvia: The core principle is that strong desire fuels the willpower necessary for achievement. Half-hearted efforts yield half-hearted results. Sometime we hide our own deep desires from ourselves, and this is one way of uncovering them.*

*Tobias: Is it okay to initially lack complete clarity?*

*Sylvia: Absolutely. Saying "I don't know, so I must not be worthy" is a fallacy.*

*Not knowing always precedes knowing – it's the essence of life's exploration, of self-discovery. Experimentation is key. Don't rely solely on your conscious mind, which is laden with preconceptions that distort your perception. There might be many things you enjoy but have ruled out due to assumptions or external influences. To expand your life, you need to open your mind to more possibilities,* gather experiences, and then refine your desires based on that knowledge.

Clarity in defining your goals is valuable, but strive to ground them in experience as much as possible. Don't be afraid to try new things, even if they don't resonate with you in the end. The process of discovery is just that — a journey of exploration, not a relentless pursuit of predetermined likes and dislikes.

## The Alchemy of Acting: Body, Mind, and the Expressive Whole

*Tobias:* The power of experience resonates deeply with what I explored in my book, *The Wizard's Way*. Einstein, Gandhi, Feynman — these titans all emphasized the primacy of firsthand experience. Reading and intellectualizing are certainly valuable, but true understanding hinges on lived experience. You can read about riding a bike all day, but only by getting on one do you really learn to ride a bike.

*Sylvia:* Precisely! It connects to what we discussed earlier about repetition. Doing is the key. In our internet age, we've fallen into the trap of thinking that thought alone suffices. It's crucial to integrate the body, the emotion, the living experience.

*Tobias:* There's a theory that consciousness is shaped, maybe even created, by that interplay of brain and body. It comes from the interplay between thought (brain) and feeling (body).

Let's shift gears a bit. I'm drawn to what I call "fully embodied" people. These people seem to be wholly connected, living in every cell of their bodies. You can just sense the vibrancy of their beings! I think this is one of the things that draws us to many celebrities — pop stars like Taylor Swift and Beyoncé come to mind.

That's in stark contrast to most of us, who seem disembodied, existing solely in their heads. Too many people today seem to use their bodies only as a carrying mechanism for their heads. Their bodies deteriorate even as their minds continue to work — but

## Chapter 9: Becoming the Change

*they're not as sharp as they could be. I see them and think, "Move! Get reconnected to your body!"*

*Sylvia: I have a term for that, for your "fully embodied person": somatic intelligence.*

*Tobias: I like that.*

*Sylvia: It's distinct from IQ, a measure of intellectual capacity. Somatic intelligence, akin to emotional intelligence, is about awareness through feeling.*

*Tobias: So, would it be accurate to say it's about experiencing the world beyond abstract intellectual concepts?*

*Sylvia: Yes, through embodied feeling. For example, how do you know you're sad? Is it a thought, or do you feel it somewhere in your body?*

*That's the question – how do you know you're angry? Where do you feel it? Some people live unconsciously reactive lives, their bodies reacting without their minds ever registering the "why."*

*Tobias: They're unaware of their movement and feelings.*

*Sylvia: They just act, propelled by unconscious reactivity. They don't consider feeling, though their bodies certainly do feel. Athletes exemplify a different facet of being embodied – they possess a deep awareness of their bodies.*

*But true embodiment extends beyond physical control and awareness. It encompasses how emotional energy is held in the body due to various psychological issues. Transforming this energy often involves movement, breath-work, and sometimes sound therapy.*

*Tobias: These elements can certainly enhance any self-awareness practices. They're valuable tools for self-discovery — which is why I enjoy your workshops so much. They remind me of my training as an actor so many years ago, which initially baffled me. Lying on the floor, imagining myself floating on clouds, or remembering a moment when I cried as a child – what did that have to do with acting? Back then, I couldn't grasp the importance of self-exploration for an actor.*

*Actor training has two facets. One focuses on immediate onstage response – your character's desires colliding with obstacles presented by another character in the here and now — the essence of dramatic tension. We train our voices and bodies to express that more effectively than the average person.*

*The other delves deeper – who am I as an actor? What do I want to express of myself through this drama? Am I a bass or a fiddle, a house cat or a lion? Who am I, what do I bring to this role that no one else can, and how can I best express it in this particular moment, through the actions of this particular character?*

*Sylvia: Or should you allow the subconscious to guide movement, voice, and expression for a richer experience?*

*Tobias: Ultimately, that's the goal of acting, achieved in different ways by different actors. But all successful actors must be sensitive to that magical moment when the character clicks, when they feel a certain way and know how to express it. They become their instrument – the entire package of body, mind, and emotions. Are they tense? Angry?*

*Sylvia: I suspect that someone could reach the same destination using a more mechanical approach.*

*Tobias: Precisely. When you're angry, you act in a certain way. If you act in that way, you feel anger! However they arrive there, the expression must feel genuine. Authenticity in the result is more important than the journey you use to get there.*

*Sylvia: Indeed. Some actors work from an internal starting point, building outward. Would you agree?*

*Tobias: Absolutely. I think of it as either working inside-out or outside-in – or maybe a combination of the two. The result is key. The Actor's Studio and Lee Strasberg were famous for their "sense memory" exercises. Actors had to recall past emotional experiences to recreate the feeling in a scene.*

*Others, like my friend Bobby Lewis, scoffed at such methods. He believed that full immersion in the character's present situation, the conflict they were portraying on stage, in the here and now,*

## Chapter 9: Becoming the Change

would evoke the appropriate emotions. Emotional baggage from the actor's own life wasn't all that necessary.

## Embodiment and the Expressive Journey

*Tobias:* Laurence Olivier's process exemplifies the "outside-in" approach to acting. After reading a script, he would sit and study himself in the mirror, experimenting with makeup and prosthetics until he achieved a physical transformation that sparked the corresponding emotional state within him.

"Once I get the nose right, the rest just falls into place."

*Sylvia:* Fascinating. The key, regardless of how you get there, is to achieve that state of "fully embodied expression." Both Olivier and actors who delve deeply into emotional recall are ultimately feeling the character intellectually, physically, and emotionally in the present moment. Their onstage expression resonates with authenticity, and authenticity is definitely what's important. When someone is performing, most audiences can instantly pick up if it's disingenuous.

*Tobias:* Feeling is the vital ingredient. Acting styles and techniques have certainly evolved throughout history. The 19th century actors like Edwin Booth, whom I call "declaimers," employed a codified set of poses and gestures for specific emotions. The "star" held center stage, surrounded by a semi-circle of supporting actors. They utilized their voice, body, and passion, but their expression differed vastly from the naturalism we see in contemporary Tennessee Williams or Edward Albee plays. I've seen operas today where this older style of acting still seems to be common.

*Sylvia:* An interesting comparison can be drawn to Indian dance storytelling. Each posture conveys a specific meaning, weaving an entire narrative. Without comprehending the language of these hand gestures, facial expressions, bodily movements, and even walking styles, the audience would have a much harder time figuring out what the gist of the storyline might be.

*Tobias:* Precisely. And I'm certain there are dancers within that tradition who, while executing the motions, evoke such a depth of feeling in themselves and their audiences that it resonates on a profound level. They're fully invested, embodying the story, and others who seem to just go through the motions.

I remember experiencing something similar in my college dance classes. Having had some prior dance experience, but not a lot, I found myself struggling in modern dance and ballet classes. Learning specific dance moves and practicing gestures and movements one by one felt unnatural, and for a while, I lost the fluidity and expressiveness I once had. Then, one day, something changed. The instructor called me out and said, "There it is! Do that again!" The vocabulary of movements I had meticulously learned and rehearsed finally clicked, and I could translate them into true, flowing expression again!

Sylvia: Exactly. When we are learning a new performance skill we often have to go through the motions and "Fake it till you make it." Once you have integrated the skill, then you can relax into its expression.

Learning a new language offers a similar parallel. You acquire individual words, but true fluency emerges only by immersing yourself in the culture. Suddenly, you find yourself not just comprehending the language but speaking it on an intuitive level. This visceral connection resonates with the process of behavior change.

Tobias: Absolutely. And all of this about acting and dance reflects what you've been telling me about how to change yourself. The actor and dancer work with full mind, body and emotion in order to portray the character. When it all finally clicks, it feels like magic! We can use those techniques to transform ourselves in real life.

In the theater, we like to rehearse a play for at least three weeks before we feel like it's ready for an audience. It takes that long for us to really "become" the characters we play, and be able hold onto that character for the two hours or so that the play lasts.

Sylvia: Yes, a period of focused effort, every day over a period of several weeks is necessary. The specific duration can vary, but consistency within a 24-hour period is key. It doesn't hinge on rigidly adhering to a set time frame, like "Oh no, I didn't meditate for the full 20 minutes!"

Tobias: Exactly.

Sylvia: The focus is on mindful engagement, even if it's for a shorter period. Being truly present in the experience, even for a brief time, carries more impact than simply going through the motions on autopilot. Fully inhabit the intention, the motion and the emotion — avoid being on autopilot.

## The Art of Attention: Cultivating Mindfulness in Daily Life

Tobias: As you know, for many years I was part of the teaching team at the McBride Magic and Mystery School. We used a phrase, when teaching our magic masterclass students: "Practice does not make perfect. Perfect practice, over a period of time, is what truly makes a great performer." If I do the move in a way that it flashes, but gets from beginning to end anyway, and I do it that way a thousand times, I've taught myself to do it wrong. But if I'm careful to make sure it's right the first time, and every time after that, well then I've trained myself to create something magical. Practice, imbued with mindfulness, is the key to refinement.

I think that applies everywhere, but outside the performing arts, we don't talk a lot about practice.

Sylvia: Mindfulness is essential in order to create in a masterful way. How can we be fully present in each moment?

What disrupts our presence? What stray thoughts or emotional triggers pull us out of the moment and into reactivity? What are our emotional pressure points — sadness, anger, frustration? We all have a default emotional state linked to past traumas, even if mild. The human experience is inherently fraught with challenges.

Tobias: Think about road rage. We overreact to reckless drivers because we've had some negative driving experience ourselves. It's instinctual — a fight or flight response. You could say that about me when I'm behind the wheel. I catch myself overreacting, and immediately wonder where that came from.

*Sylvia:* Yes, mastering our reactivity is a powerful tool for transforming our consciousness.

*Tobias:* Precisely. But how do we achieve this mastery?

*Sylvia:* As I said at the beginning of this discussion, mindfulness is a cornerstone practice.

*Tobias:* Could you offer a definition and a brief exercise?

*Sylvia:* Let's keep it simple. Don't just go through the motions. In Buddhist traditions, mindfulness is cultivated through setting intentions. For example, the Bodhisattva vow emphasizes non-harming. This requires constant evaluation of our actions – do they cause harm? Mindfulness is the tool that allows us to consistently uphold this vow.

Let's say you truly desire to cultivate inner peace. You make a 20-day commitment to mindfulness practice around that desire. This is mindfulness – consciously directing your attention, preventing distractions, and maintaining focus.

*Tobias:* So, it's a dedication to aligning intention, mind, and action.

*Sylvia:* Exactly. Mindfulness isn't about tossing trash out the window while proclaiming your love for the Earth. There's a disconnect there, a lack of coherence. Our actions, thoughts, beliefs, and values must be congruent. If you value health, indulging in cheesecake wouldn't be considered mindful self-care.

*Tobias:* Of course, we all make mistakes. Sometimes we slip up.

*Sylvia:* Yes, And I think it's important that we maintain compassion for ourselves because we're only human. Apologies to cheesecake lovers, but the point is, how do we bridge the gap between our aspirations and our behaviors? Mindfulness applied to spiritual growth might involve cultivating peace or truthfulness.

*Tobias:* I recall reading about mindfulness and consistency in the book **Atomic Habits**. The author suggests replacing generic

## Chapter 9: Becoming the Change

resolutions like "daily gym visits" with specific triggers. For instance, every time you pass a particular tree, you do three push-ups. This creates a prompt, a cue for mindful action.

Sylvia: Absolutely. For some, a calendar can be a mindfulness trigger. Schedule daily tasks at specific times, So that you don't have to rely on your memory to get started on habit.

Integrating tasks with our body clock also strengthens their hold. It's easier to establish routines.

Tobias: Thankfully, my online calendar provides audible reminders. A chime can prompt you to write, or take a well-deserved break.

But responding to those prompts is crucial, as you mentioned earlier. It's true that commitment for a month fosters lasting change, whereas getting soft on your intention and not doing what you said you were going to diminishes its effectiveness.

## The Alchemy of Success: Setting Goals and Embracing the Mission

Sylvia: Once you're really clear on what your mission is, everything arranges itself around that central fact. However, if you've got a big mission, it can feel daunting, And feelings of overwhelm can diminish your confidence, direction and effectiveness. At this point, it's best to break the entirety into achievable goals. Make goals bite-size, and before you know it success will be yours. Striving for achievable goals at this stage is paramount. Don't set yourself up for disappointment.

Tobias: Agreed. Don't write unrealistic scripts. Start small and celebrate exceeding expectations. Set a low bar on your way to achieving the high one.

Just as an example, I advise my aspiring magician students to set high goals, to keep their aspirations high, but break them into smaller, achievable goals.

## The Performer's Edge

*Let's say your goal is to earn $100,000 annually just by performing magic. Currently, you bring in $20,000. That's roughly $1,600 per month, moving to $8,300 per month. Put that way, it seems daunting. But can you envision a scenario where you increase your earnings to $1,840 next month? That's a 15% monthly increase. Perhaps you can get there by securing one additional gig each month, or just be raising your fees per show by that much.*

*Sylvia: That's attainable. It wouldn't be an overwhelming challenge.*

*Tobias: Exactly. The following month, can you manage another 15% bump, to $2,116? Keep it up, and by year's end, you'll be remarkably close to your initial target. But if you fixate on reaching $100,000 from your current $20,000 baseline, the gap appears insurmountable. Your subconscious resists.*

*The 15% monthly increase feels achievable – one extra gig, a slight price hike – something tangible to work towards and believe that you will achieve. That approach works, provided you persevere. Many students have reported remarkable success with this method. The key is setting goals you genuinely believe in, breaking them into easily achievable blocks, and persisting.*

*Sylvia: Absolutely, goals you can believe in.*

*Consider sales techniques for a moment. There are three primary approaches. 'What' describes a product's features: "a compact yet powerful device with crystal-clear recordings and a 150° ultra-wide-angle lens." 'How' focuses on functionality: "When you put it above your door, it will swivel, and give you a 360 view of your porch and yard." But the most inspiring approach speaks to the "why" – how the product will improve your life. "You'll sleep safe and secure, knowing who and what is approaching your home." That's the mission statement.*

*Tobias: The product's core purpose.*

*Sylvia: Not just the product itself. You need an even broader concept. What's the driving force behind your NGO, your startup, your life – that mission is the clarion call. It should inform every*

## Chapter 9: Becoming the Change

decision. A truly inspiring mission, one that resonates and garners support, is a recipe for success. Genuine commitment fuels action, and that's what impacts the psyche.

*Tobias:* The startup world certainly exemplifies this. Companies with clear missions are both more focused and more adept at pivoting when their initial product falters. Take YouTube, for instance. Did you know they started as a dating app, facilitating video introductions? When that concept failed to gain traction, they pivoted to becoming a general video-sharing platform. Their core product, "video sharing made easy," proved ideal for a much wider audience than the dating niche, and competition in that space was minimal.

*Sylvia:* And the evolution is still aligned with their larger core mission.

*Tobias:* Precisely. Their success stemmed from that, not their initial product idea.

*Sylvia:* We can't always predict how our grand ideas will unfold. But we can define our mission, our North Star. If one path proves unsuitable, we must be prepared to adapt. We need agility – trim the sails, shift gears, be nimble. There are countless approaches to tackling climate change, for example. Perhaps you initially considered solar energy.

*Tobias:* But perhaps, for a time, solar becomes impractical due to cost or to manufacturing shifting overseas. So, we explore wind power, but face NIMBY (Not In My Backyard) resistance. The ultimate goal, however, remains constant — reducing carbon emissions to save the planet. We can pursue that in many different ways.

*Sylvia:* Perhaps there's a way to reduce emissions and still preserve the planet, if we approach the issue from different angles.

*Tobias:* Our objective is to reverse climate change. Maybe geothermal energy becomes the answer, or perhaps public education on waste reduction proves most effective. There are countless possible strategies. It may turn out that no single strategy will work, but some combination of them will.

*Sylvia:* But with that clear objective – "I want to help combat climate change"...

*Tobias:* "I want to cool the planet down a bit. How can I contribute most effectively to that? What can I create or participate in to make a real difference?"

*Sylvia:* It all comes down to personal responsibility. There's no waiting for a savior. We, each of us, must find our own solutions and apply ourselves towards their actualization.

## The Power of Why: Uncovering the Soul of a Mission

*Tobias:* At Your Magic, one of our core principles is "technology alone won't do it; we have to change minds." But how do we affect such a shift? I have examples from acting and performance magic, but you work more directly with your work as coach and therapist.

*Sylvia:* That takes us into the essence of mission and why it is so important. Remember our earlier discussion about goals? It's not just the immediate goal, but the underlying purpose that truly ignites passion. How can we elevate mission creation to encompass a grander vision, a larger vessel for the dream?

*Tobias:* Precisely. And how do we discover that? That's why I find your "What do you want?" exercise so valuable. By repeatedly asking ourselves "What do you want?" we force introspection.

*Sylvia:* It's about achieving clarity. Someone might initially say, "Health." Each subsequent "What do you want?" deepens the exploration, connecting with their true desires and externalizing them, fostering a deeper commitment.

*Tobias:* When working with creative minds – magicians, actors, and the like — I use something similar that I call the "Why Game." It resembles a child's relentless curiosity.

"Mommy, why is the sky blue?"

## Chapter 9: Becoming the Change

*Sylvia: "Because of this and this and this."*

*Tobias: "Why?"*

*Sylvia: "Because light reflects and bends in a certain way..."*

*Tobias: "Why?"*

This playful exchange continues, eventually reaching a more profound truth, or exceeding the parent's knowledge. The relentless "Why?" either leads to a frustrated "Because I said so," or unveils the core reasons, the genuine visions, the essence of "why we do this."

I dislike the dismissive response, because it's a form of giving up. The "Why Game" transcends superficial answers. We seek the mission, the true vision, the heart of the matter – what we truly care about, yet often avoid articulating.

Sylvia: Indeed, it's easy to get caught up in superficialities.

Tobias: We settle for easy answers. But those games force us to look a bit deeper.

Sylvia: A deeply felt mission makes a world of difference in any organization. Commitment naturally varies among members. When an organization strengthens its mission focus, some will be more affected than others. However, everyone benefits from the positive ripple effect. The level of "buy-in" may differ, but the impact remains. When people are dedicated to the mission, they are more likely to put their full selves into the task of bringing it into fruition when it's just a job, it doesn't mean anything except for money.

Tobias: I consider myself fortunate in terms of employee buy-in for the companies I've run, perhaps due to them being theater based. Nobody gets into theater to get rich. The driving force is presenting the show to an audience, being onstage, and the inherent value of contributing to a successful production. That surpasses financial compensation. Actors rehearse outside of scheduled hours, alone or together, even when their union might not endorse it. The attitude becomes, "I need to excel. I'll rehearse at home. I'll do things people in other businesses wouldn't because for me it's not really about the paycheck. It's about the opportunity to do this thing."

Sylvia: There's nuance to that. Many across diverse industries work unreasonable overtime, exceeding their hourly expectations. This seems ingrained in certain business cultures. Being an entrepreneur holds a certain charm — partly because you make your own choices.

Tobias: True. The attitude may be more prevalent in entrepreneurial startups, where people aren't there solely for a paycheck. They're there because they're excited about being part of this new thing.

Working in a factory setting of a big corporation, like General Motors, might be different.

Sylvia: That's where mission becomes crucial.

Tobias: Consider Toyota's transformation. They went from producing undesirable "tin cans" to becoming the world's leading automaker.

Sylvia: They instilled a sense of purpose, an excitement about their mission, in every factory worker.

Tobias: Exactly. When you work for Toyota, your job is about innovation. Finding new ways to create excellence every day. Tightening a bolt might seem trivial, but after thousands of repetitions, your unique perspective might spark a valuable improvement. Every worker has the power to stop the line and propose a better way. Their commitment to the mission has fostered a mindset of always making things better, and not of simply putting in time and collecting a paycheck. Listening to every employee's feedback and ideas fosters a sense of being respected, which is more effective than treating people like cogs in a machine.

It's a stark contrast to some of the traditional American factory workers' mentality, where they are there to put in hours and collect a paycheck, but have no real buy-in to the mission of the corporation. In fact, they might well feel that the corporation is

## Chapter 9: Becoming the Change

their adversary, only interested in squeezing maximum work from them for minimal cost.

## The Art of Listening: A Vital Link to Success

*Sylvia: Respect is one of the cornerstones of motivation.*

*Tobias: Absolutely. There are many ways to inspire and integrate people into the vision.*

*Sylvia: Treating people well, valuing their opinions and ideas – these are fundamental principles. Many corporations struggling today are failing to heed the voices of their employees. They prioritize the agendas of their top executives, usually driven by the bottom line.*

*Tobias: The situation we're seeing today at Boeing is a great example of this. Assembly line workers, encouraged to flag problems, were then disregarded or even terminated for being trouble makers. Their mission – excellence and safety – clashed with the executive team's focus on profitability.*

*Sylvia: Companies are like living organisms, and if all parts aren't healthy and happy, the entire company suffers.*

*Tobias: Listening is paramount — which circles back to my acting metaphor. The most challenging lesson for most actors is to truly listen to their scene partners when they are performing. You have to really listen if you want to have genuine, believable reactions instead of simply waiting for your turn to speak.*

*Sylvia: It's akin to listening to the somatic body of your business.*

*Tobias: The most captivating performances occur when actors listen intently. It's that immediate response that holds the power — revealing the authentic person beneath the mask. When we speak, we often don a mask, projecting how we think we are perceived, how we appear. True listening happens when we drop the mask, and fosters a two-way exchange, a vital feedback system. Without this feedback, it's like faulty data collection in a business. Without accurate data sets, how can informed decisions be made?*

*Sylvia:* Precisely. Inability to listen equates to missing critical feedback, essentially being absent from the conversation.

Therefore, we must address our reactivity to correction. Instead of perceiving another point of view as judgment, what if we viewed it as a thanks for helping me succeed?

*Tobias:* I've learned to appreciate it when someone corrects me. It saves me from future embarrassment, and contributes to success. However, I haven't always been this way. I had to learn.

For instance, when I produce and direct a show, I make a point of being present at every performance. This fosters unity within the company. My presence isn't about being the boss; it's about offering an external perspective, providing feedback and support to the rest of the team.

Not only that, but sometimes a discussion with a member of the cast or crew winds up showing us all some new depth or direction that will make the show stronger. It's as much my job to draw those insights out as it is to share my own. This inclusivity strengthens the collective effort.

*Sylvia:* "Showing up" encompasses various aspects – physical presence, professional conduct, emotional and psychological investment, perhaps even mentor-ship. Fully "showing up" makes a world of difference.

## Getting Into Character From the Outside In

Have you ever wondered how actors manage to understand and portray characters who are vastly different from who they really are? Here's a small sample, an exercise, that I've taught, and used myself.

I imagine you sitting in a chair as you read this. As you sit there, take a moment to close your eyes and just breathe. In reality, you take in and release air through your nose or mouth, but try and imagine you can breathe in and out of every part of your body. Toes, feet, legs, abdomen,

## Chapter 9: Becoming the Change

everywhere, bit by bit. As you continue to breathe, pay attention to where you feel your center of awareness to be. For many of us, it is in our heads, because our eyes, ears and brains are in the head.

This is an abstract concept, and may be difficult to fully comprehend right away. Think about the you that commands the rest of you. If we could take you apart into pieces without damaging anything, which part would hold the 'real' you? If you don't fully get this right away, it's okay. Just make believe.

If you continue to pay attention, you can relocate that sense of center into other parts of yourself. Sometimes if you imagine that you can take a big breath directly into the part where your center is, you can use the exhale of that breath to move it. Imagine yourself centered in your heart for a few breaths. How does that feel? Perhaps this will remind you of someone you know — a warm hearted, loving individual. Or maybe it helps you remember a moment when you naturally felt this heart-centered way of being. Try centering in your stomach, your crotch, your neck, and all of your other parts. Pay attention to how you feel in each case.

Now, choose one that is not the one you began with, not the one you are most accustomed to. Spend some time breathing in and out from that new center. Try taking a short walk as you maintain this center, and notice how it changes things, if it does.

As you continue to breathe, pay attention to your face. We all carry a particular "mask" face with us when we're not paying attention to our face or reacting to something happening near us that alters our emotions, or as we react to someone we are near. What was the expression on your face before you started this exercise, as you were just sitting and reading? Experiment by changing your "mask face" as you continue to breathe. Make a face of joy, one of sorrow, of disgust — any emotion you can think of. But keep breathing from that center place you've chosen. Do you know someone who is always frowning? Someone who laughs easily, and has persistent smile lines on their faces? Try making your face look like theirs. When you find one new mask face you're comfortable with, lock it in place and keep breathing. Relax into this state, and notice how you feel.

Maintaining your new sense of center and new mask, pay attention to your internal rhythm. Most of us have a subconscious rhythm that is with us all the time. Take a quiet moment and see if you can't find yours. Dum, dum, dum, dum… there will be a particular rate that just feels right, and if you pay attention, you'll see that you think and move in harmony with that rhythm. It governs the way you move, speak, and even think. So, what is yours? Whatever rhythm seems most natural, try altering it. Faster, slower, steady or syncopated — try a number of different internal rhythms, all the time maintaining the center for your breath and the new face mask you are holding. This can feel like a lot to deal with the first few times you try it. It gets easier when you've done it a few times.

We can take this further. Take a few moments, and start walking around and exploring the space you are in, keeping the new sense of where you are centered, new face and new internal rhythm happening. If you're in a space with other people, notice how they are responding, and notice your own thoughts about them and about what is happening in the room. You might find yourself noticing and feeling things about people and your environment that you don't normally notice.

These are just a few of the possible steps we can take in order to shift our personas and inhabit different characters. For many of us, there comes a moment when this new character seems to "snap in," and it becomes easy to "be" them. You might find yourself thinking different thoughts than you are accustomed to, relating to your environment in different ways. This is the magic of acting. It also has uses for the rest of us.

I remember using something similar to try and understand those who were very different from myself while I lived in New York City. Subways are often crowded, and people go out of their way not to make eye contact — which makes the subway a perfect place for people watching. I have a distinct memory, one day, of sitting facing a heavyset black woman who had several bags with her, and was slumped back against the seat, almost in the position you might take in an easy chair if you were napping. She did not look happy. She may have been napping, or nearly so. My first thought was a negative judgment, but then I

## Chapter 9: Becoming the Change

thought, "Let me see what it might feel like to be her." I slumped in the same position, copied her facial expression, and imagined carrying around as much body weight as she did, along with all those bags — and found myself thinking completely different thoughts about the other people around us on the subway car, about where I might be going, what I'd have to deal with when I got there, etc. In just seconds I went from judging the woman to empathizing with her as she was. I may have been completely wrong both times, but the process certainly shifted my own view, and provided me insights I would never have had if I had stayed comfortable within my own customary persona.

What's the point of all this? Well, there are several.

First: If you learn to mimic or mirror other people's ways of being, the things that make them who they are, you may be able to understand them better, and communicate more effectively with them. I'm not suggesting, as they do in some NLP courses, that you try and perfectly mirror someone you're talking with in order to manipulate them during the conversation you're having. However, by observing and "getting into" the experience of their physicality before you're in conversation, you may very well discover insights and empathy for them and the way they think that will aid in your communication. We all tend to relate better to people who are more like ourselves than we do with strangers.

Second: When you learn to get inside other people's personas in this way, you're also learning to shift your own persona. There's a magical moment for an actor when a character "clicks in," and you really feel yourself becoming that person. Their strengths become your strengths. The things they fear become your fears. Their preferences become your own. Many times, this can help you expand your own self image, discover things within yourself you hadn't been aware of, and add to your personal power.

So — think of one of your personal role models, someone you really want to be more like. Find video of them in conversation or speaking before audiences. Watch the way they move and speak. Notice their resting "face mask." Can you copy it? Can you use the actors' techniques described above to get yourself into their persona, or something like it? How does that feel? Can you manage to stay in that persona for a few minutes, or hours? How does that change your day?

Third: When you wake up in the morning, you can ask yourself, "Who am I today?" Take a few minutes and adjust your physicality, your inner rhythms, your facial expression. Perhaps you want to adjust the way you speak — and start your day in this new persona. "Today, I'm Steve Jobs." (Look out co-workers!). Maybe your idol is Bob Iger, longtime CEO of Disney. Maybe it's Taylor Swift, or Ben Franklin, or Michelle Obama! Who are your heroes? Remember, nothing but your own comfort zone is preventing you from taking any of this on. Dare to be different, if only for a short while.

Perhaps the answer isn't in finding a hero, *per se*, but more in knowing the beliefs that limit you, and finding someone who either has a different set of beliefs, or who is no longer limited by those beliefs. Become that person, act as that person does for a day or two. You don't have to do it permanently — just long enough so you can discover how it feels for you to think the way they think and react around the belief you want to change. What does that feel like, in your mind and body? Can you hold on to that particular feeling and way of being without becoming the person you were emulating?

## Trauma as Change Agent

When I was about 12 years old, I experienced an electrifying transformation. I was a Boy Scout, and my troupe was on a weekend camping trip. We had hiked, set up our tents, cooked over a campfire and told ghost stories well into the evening. Now it was time to retire to our sleeping bags and get a good night's rest, so we could be ready for all the big activities of the next day. Of course, being 12 year old boys, we did nothing of the kind. Sure, we went into our tents and pretended to bed down. But an hour or so later, someone stuck his head into the tent and whispered, "Hey, we're going out for a hike without the scoutmaster. Wanna come?" We assumed that he and other adults must be asleep, so we crept out and decided to go on a little exploratory hike all on our own.

## Chapter 9: Becoming the Change

Next to the wooded area where we were camped was a farmer's pasture, surrounded by an electric fence. I had some experience with such fences, and so decided I'd demonstrate how it didn't really pose a barrier for us, if we just ducked beneath the single electric wire. Sometimes they weren't even turned on, I said. You can test them just by holding your hand flat and bouncing it…

This fence was on, and as my palm touched it, my fingers wrapped around it — and would not let go. These fences use a very high voltage, sometimes as high as 2,000-3,000 volts, but at a low amperage. That way they deliver a strong jolt when one bounces against them, but the power isn't high enough to cause any real physical damage.

I don't know how long it was before I was finally able to free myself, but it was a damp night and my feet were well grounded, so I must have danced like a crazy man for a minute or more. It seemed like ten times that long. I collapsed from exhaustion, but didn't actually pass out. My friends somehow got me back to my tent, with me telling them all the way, "I'm okay. Don't tell anyone." And they didn't.

I was mentally transformed by that single, minute-long mini-electrocution. My mind was quite certain it never wanted that experience again, and that manifested as an instant "super phobia" against touching anything metal. The pipes in the basement, for example — I could not force myself to touch them. I was even leery of small metal objects like keys. This was more than just a mild phobia, where you don't want to touch that icky slug in the garden. It wasn't a case of not wanting to touch metal, but one where I could not even force myself to do it. The phobia lasted for more than a year!

I remember finally making myself get over the phobia by forcing myself grab onto a cold radiator pipe. We lived in a house built in the 1860's, and our heat in the house was all via cast iron radiators. There was one in my bedroom, and I hadn't touched it for over a year, but one day I decided I just couldn't continue with the phobia, so I gritted my teeth and forced myself. On the first attempt, it was as though there was a force field around the radiator. My hand just would not, could not touch it. But then I managed it. Once, twice, three times. I could do it! For the next week or two, I made myself go out of the way to touch every metal or possibly electric thing I could. It took some time, but after that, I've never had the problem again.

What's the takeaway from my shocking transformation? We all have traumas, and many of them embed phobias and other restrictions into our nervous systems so deeply they can actually disable our ability to function. You can indulge your traumas and the neurosis they cause. They become a part of the reality you experience. I could actually "feel" the metal radiator pushing back against me when I got within a few inches of it. That was real — to me then — but I was able to overcome it, simply by forcing my way through. I'm not suggesting that this is true for all traumas, or all people at all times. But I do think there is always some way through. If you can't do it yourself, well that's why we have therapists!

It's important to remember that trauma we've experienced doesn't always manifest in a way that seems directly connected, not at first. Therapists know this, and they know it's important for each of us to confront our own personal traumas in our own ways. However all too often, those same therapists will spend months and years helping you through a trauma you might be able to get through as quickly as I did, just by forcing myself to touch that radiator (and pipes, and light switches, and…) again and again. My belief was strong, and embedded as deeply into my nervous system as could be. But it was possible to change it.

## Performing is Story Telling

I often work with magic students who tell me, "I'm not a story teller." Some of them don't even speak, but perform to music in a kind of magical dance. My response is always, "Of course you are. Your audience will take a story away with them, whether you're telling it in words or not. The only question is, will the story you tell be a good one? Will it be easy for them to follow? Will they care about what they remember happening? Will they even be able to remember what happened? Too often, the answer to all these questions is in the negative."

The solution I can offer is one every actor knows: use subtext. Subtext is the underlying meaning or intention beneath the surface of spoken dialogue or written text. It's the unspoken thoughts, emotions, and motivations that drive a character's words and actions. Creating and using subtext involves:

1. Uncovering the character's true feelings and desires that may contradict or deepen their explicit statements.

2. Infusing dialogue with layers of meaning through tone, body language, and subtle cues.

3. Communicating complex emotions and intentions without explicitly stating them.

Effective use of subtext allows actors to convey depth, authenticity, and complexity in their performances, enabling audiences to connect with characters on a more profound level[1][4]. It's the art of saying one thing while meaning another, creating tension between what is spoken and what is truly felt or intended.

Often, when we use subtext, it's actually a running silent dialog we play for ourselves as we perform. For a magician starting to perform a card trick, she might say, "Have a look at these cards. All the same on the back, but different on the front."

She'll spread the cards face up on the table, thinking to herself, "Here, look at the faces. Notice (as she gestures), how they're all different. Take your time. Got it? Good!" This last is said as she gathers the cards and turns them face down in her hand.

Thinking to herself (subtext), "Now who shall I have choose a card? Let's see…not you, but I'll pretend I want you to, then pull it away, like this, because I don't like you… but you, you I like, and you'll be perfect!" And she'll fan the cards, now face down, and hold them toward the person she wants to take the card.

She says, out loud, "Would you just point to any one of the cards. Make sure to point at the one you want, not one you think I want you to point to. Good. Now just pull that card out and look at it, making sure I can't see the face." To herself, she thinks, "Smile as he takes it, then turn your head away."

I think you're getting the idea, but here's the thing: We all have subtext running, almost all the time. If you take a minute and pay attention, you'll realize you have something running through your mind right now, other than the words on the page.

You might be thinking, "He wants me to stop reading for a moment? OK. Let's see…how long do I have to stop? Oh, look at the clock…I've been reading now for 10 minutes. Maybe time for a snack. No…I'm going to power through this chapter." I'm just guessing, and you might well have something entirely different running through your mind right now. But there is something there.

Most of our constant subtext isn't something we choose, but it can be. In fact, a lot of your sub-text comes from your beliefs. As an actor portraying a character, I can choose different beliefs and different subtext. "Take that! You deserved to die, sucker!" isn't something I might think, but a character I'm playing might very well think and feel exactly that.

One of the quickest ways to change at least some aspects of who you are is to choose different subtext. Actors construct different subtext for every character, and you can, too. Imagine you're at the wheel of your car and someone cuts into your lane going just a bit too fast and a bit too close to you. "You @#x*%!" immediately pops into your brain. Maybe you even say it out loud. You've just become an angry, reactive person. Suppose you consciously chose to tell yourself, "Wow. That guy must be late to work. I hope he makes it okay!" You're still startled, and still a little upset. But you have just become a different character than the person cursing the other one for their actions. And you've just turned what might have been a traumatizing situation into one where you can exercise empathy and even kindness.

## The Magic of Mindset

When I was a teenager, we lived in a large Victorian house. We had a couple of extra guest bedrooms, and my Dad would sometimes make them available to people he knew who were doing good work in the world, but had encountered rough times recently. One was

## Chapter 9: Becoming the Change

our local "minister of the streets," who among other activities, ran a youth recreation center in a rough part of town. One of the ways he maintained order and a connection with the kids there was through hosting competition level table tennis tournaments. He was an amazing player, and turned us into the same. We had a "ping pong room" on the third floor, where we often played, but once Adam moved in, we all had to up our games. No more tapping the ball back and forth forever till the other side made a mistake. Now we had to develop much faster, more highly controlled games. Every shot had some kind of spin on it, and sometimes you just had to know where that next shot was going, because you didn't really have time to "see" it.

I, somehow, became the house champion. I got good enough to beat Adam, my brother, my father and all my friends. Some of them were just as skilled and as fast, as I was. I beat them anyway. And it wasn't until I had gone off to college and not played for almost a year that I realized why.

I came home one weekend to find that my brother had been practicing while I was away. He could hit the ball harder, with more spin and control than I could. He was faster. As we warmed up, it seemed inevitable he was going to wipe the table with me. But then the game began.

Going into competition mode, everything came back to me. "I don't know how, but I'm going to win this," was the thought at the top of my mind. Sure, Tim (my brother) was faster, and his skills were amazing. But he, too, had a belief — only his was, "I can't beat Tobias." And so after a dozen or so games, I still had only lost one. It was clearly not that I was more skilled. But my belief that I would win made me go just that much further, reaching the "unreachable" shots, and making the "impossible" plays each game — and I still won.

Later in life, reflecting on this, I have to wonder: If that strong belief in my ability to win at table tennis affected my play so much, what other beliefs have I had which helped or hindered my success in life? I maintained a mostly positive attitude, and have had many successes. But I have dreams I haven't managed to reach, too. If I'm honest with myself, I expect it was more my limiting beliefs than limited ability that has held me back. It may be time for me to make some changes myself.

# Chapter 10
# Question Everything!

## Questioning Beliefs and Assumptions

Richard Feynman was a famous physicist and a boldly free-thinking character. He was one of the key contributors to the Manhattan Project, which led the US to beat the Nazis to the creation of the atomic bomb. His "Feynman Diagrams" were key to our ability to work with the mathematics of quantum mechanics. Later on he proved to be one of the greatest teachers of physics of all time. You can still watch many of his lectures, now made available on YouTube.com (just search for "Feynman") and elsewhere.

Feynman liked to tell his students, "The most important thing is not to fool yourself. And you are the easiest one to fool!" (This comes from his 1974 commencement address at Caltech, which he entitled "Cargo Cult Science.") He was speaking to budding theoretical physicists, warning them that their natural preconceptions and assumptions might well lead them astray in their struggle to work out the reality of whatever scientific frontier they might be working on.

This principle can be applied to many situations that you may encounter as you move through your life. It is especially important as we are striving to create new businesses. We might have a wonderful new idea, an ability to create something that could change society. So we look for a way to build a business around that idea, or a new product it inspires. The thinking would be, "If I create A, and know about market B, I can tailor product A to appeal to and serve market B. We'll change the world — and then we can all live happily ever after." If only it were that simple!

In fact, there are a thousand steps involved in the creation of the product, and another thousand in bringing it to market. As an entrepreneur, you need to examine and question every one of those steps. Are all of the obvious ones really necessary? What assumptions are you making, at each step, that might not hold up? Do all the results actually match up with the causes you're assuming? Or are they simply correlated phenomena, actually caused by something you haven't considered? Do you actually need step D in order to get to step E, or is that just "the way its done?" Does the "market" you seek to serve actually need or desire what you're creating? Are they feeling a pain you can resolve? If not, can you make your product so awesome they find they want it? (Think of the iPad — no one knew they needed or even wanted one, until they saw it in action!).

That all sounds a bit daunting, doesn't it? Just remember that thousands of small and large business folk have done it before you. In the words of Dr. Norman Vincent Peale, "You Can if you Think you Can."

So, if you want to change the world, it's essential that you continue to question, continue to try and find ways you might be wrong about your assumptions, and be willing to change course when you are.

## Questioning Your Assumptions with Magic

Once we understand just how tenuous our grip on reality can be, we can find it extremely useful to adopt this mantra of "Question Everything." Here's a little magic trick that demonstrates why this is so useful — and even necessary.

One of my favorite magic tricks is called "Spot Card." My version is among the simplest: The magician describes an odd artifact given him by a real wizard. He shows a card with a single "spot" on one side, two such spots on the second side, and then goes on to show three on a third(?) side and four on the fourth(?) side. But normal cards typically only have two sides, and this looks like a normal card. What could be going on here? How is the magician bending our reality?

# Chapter 10: Question Everything!

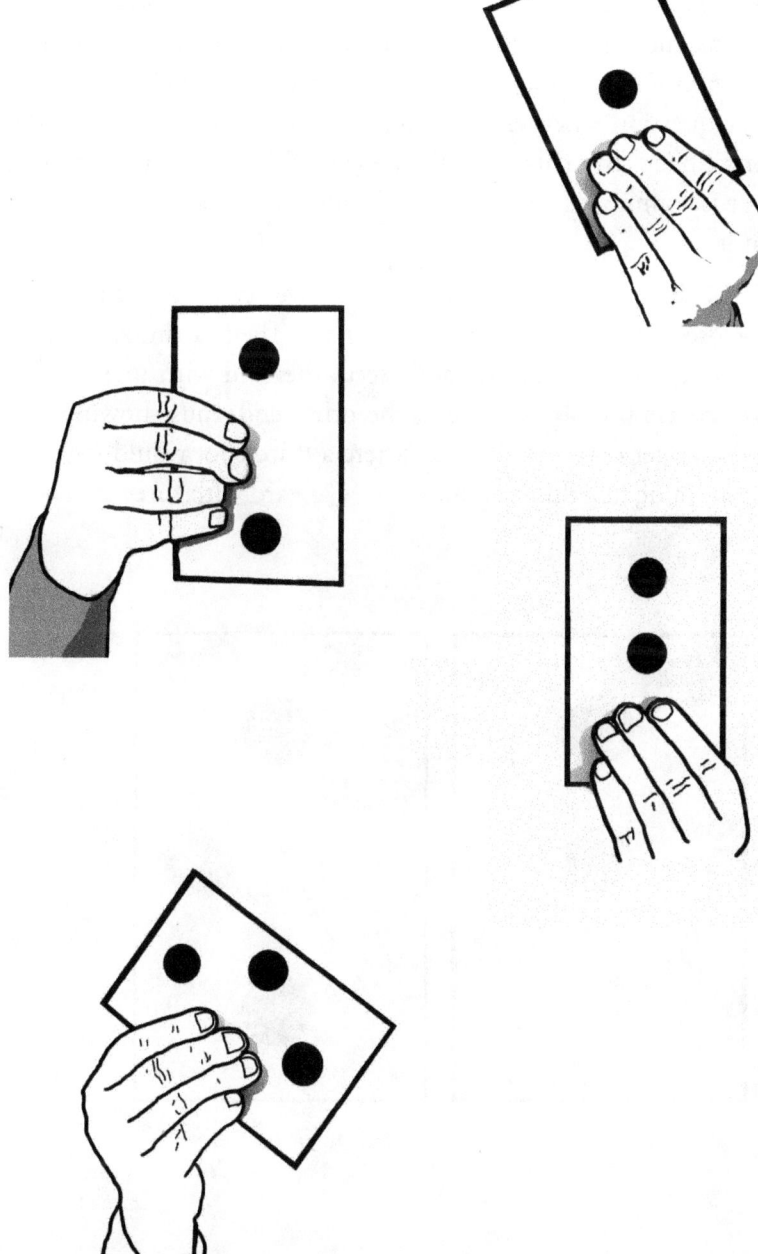

In fact, the magician is taking advantage of our need to use what Daniel Kahneman termed "fast thinking" (*Thinking, Fast and Slow* by Kahneman), which is necessary because of our need to rebuild our experienced reality many times each second. Our ability to process incoming data is limited, so we must rely on our preconceived assumptions and heuristics in order to create and make sense of our reality from moment to moment. So we see the card showing one spot, and never question whether there might be another spot behind the magician's finger. The pattern with the card showing a single spot in the center is common. It makes sense. That's what we see, and we don't question it.

In reality, the card has two dots. The one we see in the center, and another close to one end, covered by a finger. The fast thinking mind assumes the most likely image, and "sees" the card with one spot. If the finger covers the blank space at the other end, thus showing two spots and a finger covering the area where a third spot would logically appear, that same fast thinking mind "sees" a card with three spots.

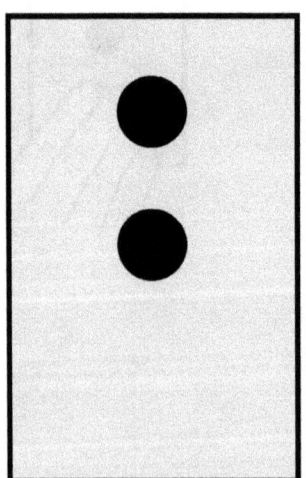 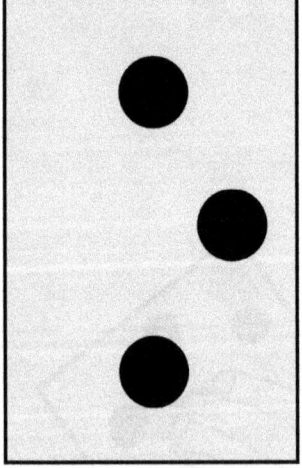

## Chapter 10: Question Everything!

We have a similar situation on the other side of the card. There are actually 3 spots, but if a finger covers one of them, and the other two are arranged just as they would be if there were only two, the mind assumes it's seeing a two spotted card. If the finger covers the blank, we "see" four spots. The magician is careful to cover the right spot or blank space as the card is turned, enabling a display of 1, 2, 3 and 4 different sides of the same card. The impossible made real!

Once we make an effort to habituate ourselves to "slow thinking," and begin questioning everything, we become more difficult to fool with such simple subterfuges. If we truly make that a habit, we begin to see what I think of as "false illusions" in many areas where we hadn't expected them. Most of what we experience is an illusion, in that it is just a model within our brain, one that accurately reflects what is out there — but a "false" illusion is one that sends a message that conflicts with the reality "out there." Optical illusions and magic tricks are examples, and part of the reason they can be such fun is that they help us realize just how our minds do fool us much of the time.

### Feynman's Computing Team

One of my favorite books is Richard Feynman's *Surely You're Joking, Mr. Feynman*. It is just a series of anecdotes from Feynman's life, but told in his own unique voice and irreverent attitude.

At one point, Feynman talks about his work at Los Alamos, during the atomic bomb project. He was in charge of their computation division, and one of the charges was to work out just exactly how much energy the bomb was likely to release when detonated. Different possible designs were being considered, and it was important to know which would be most effective.

The big problem was that the computations turned out to be extremely complex. There seemed to be no possible way of speeding them up. They figured out that existing computing machines would be able to do them, but they didn't have the machines there, and they were racing against time to make sure the US got the bomb before our enemies. Machines were ordered, but Feynman and his team didn't want to wait.

So, while there were waiting, Feynman organized a team of women with calculators. He designed the program that the computers would use, once they arrived, and the team organized themselves so that each of them could calculate one step of the program, then pass the result to the next one, who would compute her step, pass the result on, etc. This was a way to test the program before the computers arrived. As it turned out, it was also a way to speed things up, essentially a version of parallel processing that hadn't been used before. Before Feynman's system, it had taken 9 months to compute 3 problems – as I had mentioned, it was a very complex process. Using Feynman's system, they could do 9 problems in 3 months. As it turned out, the team of women using the new system could actually compute the problems almost as fast as the machines could, once they arrived and were up an running.

Feynman's rethinking of "the way it's done," and not accepting what he had been taught at face value may have been a deciding factor in the US completing the project in the time they did.

## More Magicians' Secrets

Let's examine this concept of "Question Everything" from a slightly different angle — that of a master magician practicing his craft of deception for entertainment.

Juan Tamariz, from Madrid, Spain, is a renowned magician celebrated for his expertise in card magic and his deep thinking about magical theory. Tamariz gained international acclaim when he won awards at the FISM World Championships of Magic in Paris in 1973. His books, ***The Five Points in Magic***, ***The Magic Way***, and ***Mnemonica*** explore both technique and theoretical concepts, and are studied by serious students of magic everywhere. In addition to his literary contributions, Tamariz is well known in Spanish and South American entertainment through television appearances and live performances. He co-founded the "Escuela Magica de Madrid" in 1971, which significantly impacted magic education. Known for his comedy and his intellectual approach to misdirection and performance psychology, Tamariz has inspired countless magicians worldwide.

## Chapter 10: Question Everything!

Tamariz's concept of "false solutions" or "false methods" is a key part of his approach to magic. This idea is most thoroughly explored in his book The Magic Way, which is considered one of the most important works on the theory and philosophy of stage magic. It involves deliberately leading spectators to think they have figured out how a trick is done, only to then disprove that solution, leaving them with no logical explanation for what they've witnessed. This technique is designed to create a stronger sense of impossibility and wonder in the audience's mind. The message is conveyed through the magician's behavior.

For example, in a particular card trick, the magical outcome might be explained if we believe the magician has a card "palmed," or hidden in the palm of his hand. A magician might hold the hand in a way that would indicate there might be a card hidden there — but then turn the palm to the audience as he moves through the trick. Another possible indication might be that two cards are aligned with one another but only one is shown. The other would be hidden from view, and this might be the explanation for the magic that is about to take place. The magician would handle the card with extra care, indicating it might actually be hiding another behind it, but then hand it to a spectator for a moment, making it obvious that the double card idea would be impossible. In any given routine, several of these moments where an idea of how the magic could be done are indicated, then shown to be false, will take place. Then, when the magic moment comes, it is far more amazing in the audiences' minds. The magician has been playing with our expectations all along!

Of course, the audience for a magician is a special case. They're expecting the magician to try and fool them, so they are of a mind to question everything from the start. Tamariz is playing with this mindset, wearing them out, before he does fool and delight them with his magic.

In the case of magic performances, the artist's purpose is often to force us to question all of our assumptions, and Tamariz' technique takes that a step further. Question reality, then question it again and again. Who knows, you might just discover real magic!

## Reflection and Questioning

Because we're so used to our everyday "fast thinking" experience of reality, and because that fast thinking is often necessary in order to function in the world, sometimes we need to take time out for reflection. We need to take time to stop moving, stop reacting — time just to reflect and to think slowly about what matters to you.

I hope you'll do that now. Here are a few things you might think about: Have you taken time to examine the secondary choices you're making when you make a conscious choice? Most of us think about what our friends and others will think of us for having that car, or how it will feel to sit behind the wheel. But that shiny new car comes with payments, insurance payments, safety considerations, repair costs and fuel costs. When you buy it, you're making choices about all of those things, and perhaps about effects on the environment, as well. How many of those secondary choices did you consider?

Take a little time and think about the last time you bought something that felt costly. Many times we all make decisions — especially about buying things we think we want — without considering all the effects and secondary effects, both on ourselves and on the world around us. We seldom consider all the alternatives we might have, especially when what we want is what "everyone wants."

Any good salesman will tell you that virtually all the decisions you make are made with your emotions, and then justified by reasoning. The salesman will manipulate your emotions, your subconscious, into making the decision they want you to, and you wind up purchasing something you don't really need or want. This is a good model of how our failure to question everything (go home and think it over!), can harm you in life. Learn to step away and engage your slow-thinking, more aware and rational self before making impulsive decisions! Learn to see individual actions in the context of the larger systems you are a part of. Learn to see the consequences of your actions today over time.

Interactions with our children or co-workers are a great place to start. Did someone's behavior annoy you, so you responded sharply with an insult? Take a moment and question yourself — will that response

## Chapter 10: Question Everything!

come back to haunt me? Did I just traumatize my child in a way that might affect their future? If we take the time to consider such things, we can generate two great results: First, we can learn to apologize and set things straight for the other person. This can make all the difference in your future relationship with someone you care about. Second, we can begin the process of changing ourselves so that we're less prone to such damaging behavior. But you only get the great results if you take time out to think!

I remember, in reading one of those books on how to become successful and wealthy — I think it was T. Harv Eker's *Secrets of the Millionaire Mind* — the author asked us to sit down and write about how we felt about wealthy people. I had a fairly strong belief that a lot of wealthy people got that way by taking advantage of others. As it happens, that was one of the beliefs that the author, on the next page of the book, suggested would prevent me from ever becoming wealthy! I held that belief even though I was engaged in helping clients become wealthy and successful, even while not helping myself to do those very things. If asked, I would have told you I was working on becoming more successful. In fact, the underlying belief *was* holding me back. The fact that it wasn't true was evidenced by the example of the very people I was helping!

We've talked about the ability of our conscious minds to pay attention to one thing at a time, while the subconscious can pay attention to many. Many of our techniques for changing ourselves involve ways to get conscious and sub-conscious into alignment.

I once took a workshop with Sylvia Brallier, who you met earlier in this book, in which she was teaching a shamanic technique for developing personal power. The message was that once you can let go of all of the underlying beliefs you hold — often in the subconscious — about your lack of power, and change them to confident beliefs in your own real power, you will become infinitely powerful, infinitely capable. I've certainly not reached that point in life, but I do think of the teaching and work on it a bit every day. Every time I catch myself thinking, "I can't do that, because…" I force myself to reconsider. Why not? Is that thing I perceive really holding me back? What excuses am I making? Are they real? Are there ways around them?

We've talked about the ability of our conscious minds to pay attention to one thing at a time, while the subconscious can pay attention to many. Many of our techniques for changing ourselves involve ways to get conscious and sub-conscious into alignment.

# Chapter 11
# Different Perspective, Different Reality

## A Bizarre Experience

This took place sometime in 1991. Our show, *Mask, Myth and Magic* was booked as the headlining attraction for the London Mime Festival, in London. It was my first time traveling to the U.K., and I was beyond excited! The land of King Arthur and Merlin, home to Shakespeare and the Royal Shakespeare Company, and we were going there to perform!

We were surprised when we arrived in London to hear, repeatedly, people asking, "Oh, how can you live in New York City? We hear about all the drive-by shootings and the crack epidemic. It must be awful! Aren't you frightened all the time?" That's what was making the news about New York City at the time. There was some truth to it, but those things were happening mostly in the South Bronx, not in Manhattan, where we all lived. If you've lived in New York, you're aware that the five boroughs are very much like five separate cities, each with its own culture, or to be more accurate, set of cultures. When you live in Manhattan, a trip to the South Bronx is rare.

Our show was to be at the South Bank Center, a large performing arts center not unlike the Kennedy Center in Washington, D.C. We were in one of the several mid-sized theaters there, and it was a different experience for us after the many casinos and cabarets we had performed in. We had a union stage crew for the show, and as lighting designer/production manager for the show, it was my task to work with them to set the lighting. Although we had sent our full lighting plot to them weeks before we arrived, none of the lighting or sound equipment was in place. The crew had it in mind to get in as much overtime on the night of our lighting hang and focus session as they could, and so a session I had done in several casinos in just a couple of hours wound up lasting until the wee hours of the morning. There were only a couple of hours between the end of the lighting hang and the beginning of our tech rehearsal the next morning, and the trip between our hotel and the South Bank Center would have used up half that time. I ended up sleeping for a couple of hours on a bench in one of our dressing rooms.

Everyone arrived on time, and we were a couple of hours into the technical rehearsal when it was time for a union break. It was to be 30 minutes, so I took the time to go to the men's room and freshen up. I was probably in there for 10-15 minutes at most. When I came out, it was into a different world. The halls were completely empty. This was a busy performing arts center, with probably 5 different shows preparing for performances that evening. The halls had been noisy and full of people when I went into the restroom.

But now — they were empty and silent. Very strange!

I started my walk back to our theater, and still couldn't find anyone. Where were they? Had I stepped through a time warp? Was the Twilight Zone real? Since the place seemed completely devoid of humans, I took the opportunity to explore some of the various rehearsal halls, concert halls and other parts of the building. Wherever I went, silence!

Finally, I thought to check the doors to the outside, and there, surrounding the building was a huge crowd, being held back by those London Bobbies you've seen in films. What could be happening?

I went out the doors and was quickly escorted into the crowd. It turned out there had been a bomb scare called in for the building, and there was a bomb squad inside searching every nook and cranny for a possible bomb. The IRA had set off two other bombs in London earlier that week, and they feared this might be the largest one of all.

After another hour or so, they decided it had been just a scare, and let us get back to work. That night at dinner with our sponsors, I couldn't resist asking, "So you live with these bombings and threats of bombings every day, but you think New York is the scarier place?"

That led to a discussion of how we always get comfortable with what we know, and stay uncomfortable, often frightened, by the unfamiliar. To the Londoners, IRA bombings were common and just something you had to live with. To us New Yorkers, London seemed indescribably dangerous.

## Chapter 11: Different Perspective - Different

Which leads me to an insight: Your experienced reality is largely a matter of your point of view. If you can learn to see things from different perspectives, you often find that what you had found frightening has become commonplace. Things that once looked impossible become easy, once you've done them a hundred times. That "impossible, stunning" magic trick loses all its magic the second you learn how it's done!

How is this an empowering phenomenon? The trick is to learn to examine a situation from several different perspectives immediately when you encounter it. You have one point of view, but your customer has another, and the person who delivered your product to that customer has yet another. The whole sales transaction looks one way today, but when you look back on it in a year, everyone involved will view it differently. How many arguments would be avoided if we all took a few minutes to ask for and understand the other person's point of view?

# Chapter 12
# Attention is Everything

I started this book with the assertion that all businesses succeed and fail today by their ability to create positive experiences. We want to create experiences for our employees so they'll be happy and productive. Experiences for our customers so they'll want to become long-term clients.

Charles Revson, the founder of Revlon Cosmetics understood this when he famously stated, "In the factory we make cosmetics; in the store we sell hope." You might think you're manufacturing widgets, but in fact you're in the business of creating a vision of a better life for your customers when they use those widgets.

In the world of the theater, we are clearer about our product from the start. We are creating and selling experiences unencumbered with material products. And the theatrical director is the person who is most directly responsible for adjusting those experiences to fit a particular audience.

It was the first day of my college class in directing. I was fairly sure at that point in life that directing for the theater was my real calling in life, but this was the first chance I had to take a course in directing. We weren't allowed into the course until we had completed basic acting, literature and theater history classes.

"What's your primary job as a director?" my professor asked.

"Ah…I don't know. To provide an overall vision for the play, and use the actors, set and lighting to bring that vision to fruition?"

"Good, but no."

"To run rehearsals."

"That, too…but no. Your primary job is to direct the audience's attention."

That was the biggest lesson of that course in directing. "Learn to direct attention. Attention is everything!" At any given moment, you're surrounded with hundreds of things you could pay attention to. A hundred different small things you can react to. But the one that you do pay attention to is the one you'll remember. That's the one that will actually affect your life. Especially if you're in an audience.

You are in an audience in order to experience a story. That story has a through line that will take you from its beginning to its end, and if your attention isn't on the right thing, that through line will break, and the story will break. So the director's primary job is to make sure your attention stays where it needs to in order for you to have the experience that you'll remember as the story.

As it turns out, this is true for the story you're living and calling "my life," as well. Put your attention on the right things, and you will thrive and live a powerful, fulfilled life. Put it on the wrong things, and you may end up homeless and addicted to drugs. Those are the extremes, and most of us fall somewhere in between.

Attention can be directed by others, as when we have good experiences in the theater. As a director, I have a number of tools available to me to guide my audiences' attention. The composition of the stage picture is one. The use of light is another. Movement onstage is yet another. The attention the performers give to one another directs the audience's gaze. These are just a few of my tools for directing your attention.

In life, you'll encounter many who want to direct your attention — teachers, marketers, bosses, your family — and many of those will govern your life if you let them. We each also have the ability to take control of where we place our attention. This is the true secret of success for many.

## An Experiment in Directing Attention

Here's a fun experiment. You'll need a friend and two decks of playing cards. The two decks need to have different, contrasting back designs. I like to use one that's red and one that's blue. These are easily found anywhere playing cards are sold.

To prepare, take 7 cards from one deck and 6 cards from the other. Place the rest of the cards aside. Look at the faces of the 13 cards you've

## Chapter 12: Attention is Everything

chosen, and make sure there aren't duplicates. For example, if I see the 6 of hearts twice, I take one and return it to the deck it came from, exchanging it for another card that I don't already have in my little collection.

At this point, you should have 13 cards in front of you, all different on their faces, 6 of which have blue backs, and 7 with red. Turn them face down and mix them randomly so the red and blue backs are thoroughly mixed. Up to this point, don't let your friend or audience see what's happening. When you're ready to work with your audience, place the packet of cards face down in your left hand, and you're ready to begin the process for your friend. Magicians would call this the "set up."

Sitting or standing face to face with your friend, you say, "I have a packet of 13 cards here. As you can see, they're just a random mix of different cards." You turn the cards face up and fan them so your friend can see all the different faces for a few seconds, then close the fan and turn it face down in your left hand again. Because the packet is closed up, no one will suspect the cards might have different colored backs.

"We're just going to try a simple memory test here. You'll find it almost too easy, but in the end, I think you'll also find it a bit surprising. I'm just going to deal the cards, one at a time, turning each one face up on the table. You don't have to remember the specific cards, but I want you to count how many black cards you see. Since we have 13 cards, knowing the number of blacks will also tell you how many reds. Don't try to track both things, though. It's hard to pay attention to two things at once, and you can just use simple arithmetic when we get to the end. Simple, right?"

They'll say yes, and you can begin dealing the cards, one at a time, face up, onto the table. Don't rush, and don't distract them. Make sure the backs of the cards show before each one is dealt, so that they do see the different colored backs, even though you're not calling attention to that fact. Once all the cards are on the table, ask them, "OK. How many black cards did you see?" They'll be able to tell you.

"And that means there are how many red cards?" They should be able to tell you this, as well.

"And how many cards with blue backs?"

If you started with a blue backed card on top of the pile, the likely answer will be "All of them." Otherwise, you'll probably see a look of confusion, or get an answer like "I wasn't paying attention." I've done this for friends a number of times, and they are always completely unaware that the cards have different colored backs until you show them.

Why? It's because you directed their attention to the faces of the cards, and to counting how many black cards they saw. Their eyes do see the different colored backs, but their conscious minds do not. As it turns out, for most of us, our conscious minds can pay attention to just one thing at a time. We have peripheral awareness of much that is going on around us, and that awareness colors our feelings about the thing we are paying attention to, but the real attention is focused on one thing.

## Become Your Own Director

Once you're aware that where you place your attention will determine your experience, you begin to understand how important it is for you to take control of your own attention. Have you known people who seem to place a great deal of their attention on what they see as their personal deficiencies? Perhaps they have some physical or psychological condition that's a bit out of the ordinary, and they can't seem to stop thinking and talking about it. You might know others with the same deficiencies, but who never mention them. Of the two, who do you think experiences more success?

For example, one of the most successful magicians I know is autistic. He does pay attention to his autism, and uses it as part of the story he tells in his performances. But he spends most of his time and attention on becoming a better performer and building his career as a performer. Honestly, outside of discussing his performances with him, I've never heard him talk about autism. That's simply not where he wants to put his attention, because he doesn't find it productive.

## Chapter 12: Attention is Everything

Richard Branson, famous for all the Virgin brands he has built, is also well known to be dyslexic and to have ADHD. He doesn't spend much time talking about either one, though, because he's too busy and excited about running his companies.

The message here? It's okay to acknowledge the things that limit you, but make an effort to put most of your attention on where you want to go, the things you want to accomplish. Don't let the world outside of your control make the decisions about where you'll put your attention. You have the ability to take control of this for yourself. As we mentioned in a previous chapter, "Where the attention goes, energy flows." So put your attention where you want to go! If you're on the leadership team of your company, stay focused on your mission and goals. Take care of the challenges, but know that the more important use of your attention and energy is, as they say, keeping your eye on the prize!

*Chapter 13: The Art of Practice*

# Practice is a Super Power

Let's bust some myths about practice.

But first, what is practice? For the most part, it is the process of repeating a skill you want to master many, many times. There's a notion, first put forth (as far as I'm aware) in a 1993 study by Anders Ericsson, that it takes 1,000 hours of practice to achieve mastery. Ericsson doesn't put this forth as a hard number, but an average. Malcolm Gladwell popularized the idea in his book ***Outliers: The Story of Success***, which came out in 2008. The 'thousand hour principle' may be true, but actual numbers will vary depending on innate talent and the kind of skill being mastered. It should also be noted that the figure is for "mastery," and in fact it generally takes a lot less practice to become competent at most skills.

The one thing in common with all these accounts is that practice — lots of repetition — is involved. You can think of practice as training your nervous system through repetition of a particular skill, done as perfectly as you can each time, until you can do it without having to think about it. Apparently when you repeat the same action, the same set of neurons respond in the same order, and eventually a pathway is built up around that action. The more you repeat the thing, the stronger the pathway.

Here's our first fallacy, our first myth to be busted. Practice alone does not make you perfect at a skill. Only perfect practice makes you perfect. Repeating the wrong thing won't help — it will make the wrong thing permanent. As a simple example, I've seen hundreds of magicians who have practiced a skill for many hours, but they've practiced the skill they are trying to master incorrectly, resulting in performances which essentially teach their audiences how a trick is done, instead of really fooling them. The card "hidden" in the palm of the hand flashes for just an instant, or is held in a way that makes the hand appear unnatural — and the illusion is destroyed. Every time. Bad practice!

Good practice, on the other hand, is done with one's full attention. You're not just repeating the move again and again, but you are repeating it while paying attention to just what you are doing. Looking at it, or having others look at it, from many different angles. Doing it at different speeds. Doing it while speaking or listening, then checking the result, again and again, until it does seem perfect — and then a hundred times more until you no longer have to think about how the skill is done.

With many skills, there are different levels of the skill that you can only discover through extensive practice. Once you become competent at one level, you might find there are further nuances that can improve the skill further — but only if you're willing to put in another few hundred hours of practice!

The need for good practice is essential in all of the performing arts. Only once all of the skills are fully practiced is the musician ready to play music, the dancer ready to dance expressively, or the magician ready to put the magic in front of an audience. It is essential for the athlete who wishes to excel. Honestly, practice is the magical method we can use to master any skill.

Here's a secret about practice: practice itself is a skill. Find something you want to learn and start practicing it. The more you practice, the better you'll become at it! By building up your ability to practice one thing, you'll find it much easier to start practicing another.

## Rehearsal

As performers, we practice our skills, but we rehearse our performances. The difference being that a skill is something that is usually short, and later becomes a part of a performance. I might practice a particular way of hiding a coin in palm, but I rehearse the magical routine I perform for an audience, which might include that particular technique, along with other elements. I practice playing scales and chords on my guitar, but I rehearse songs, many of which might use the techniques I've practiced. As an actor, I might practice vocal skills and dialects, but I rehearse the sketch or play that might use those skills in.

How does this translate into the world of work and personal relationships? Perhaps it might be clearer using sports as our example.

## Chapter 13: The Art of Practice

We practice shooting baskets, rebounding and the like — but we rehearse plays we want to be able to execute when we play the game. Both involve repetition, but the practice part can be repeated a hundred times in a single session, while the rehearsal probably doesn't take place as often.

Like practice, in its early stages, rehearsal is where we work out the difficulties, finding better and better ways of achieving whatever it is we are rehearsing. Is it a talk you'll give at a friend's wedding? The serious talk you need to have with your kids? A presentation at your next business meeting? Practice and rehearsal can make a huge difference in the quality of each of these situations.

If you've gone to a business or a scientific conference, you've probably experienced a lot of terrible presenters, and just a few good ones. The terrible presenters might be giving out terrific information, but it doesn't get through. They know their subject, but have no idea of how to present it, and often couldn't even tell you exactly why they are sharing it with you. More often than not, they read the presentation from notes or from their PowerPoint slides.

However, the rare great presenter (watch TED talks for some great examples) has no need of notes. Their backup materials add to their talks. The talks tell stories and are filled with personal experience and emotion. They look and feel as though the person is thinking the thoughts as they come to them — but if you see the same talk a dozen times, it barely changes from time to time. You leave that conference remembering the one or two great talks you heard, and immediately forgetting all the others.

Why? Well there are many things that go into making a presentation great, but perhaps the biggest one is that the speaker has rehearsed the talk many, many times. You can find a number of Steve Jobs' talks, given when new products were launched on YouTube and other sites. The talks feel as though they are just "off the cuff," and Jobs is speaking in the moment. In fact, he would rehearse them for a week with a team of writers and directors in order to make sure they did feel that way.

When rehearsing, you go through an initial period where you're just trying to get through the presentation. Then there's a second phase where you realize that what you wrote doesn't sound like natural speech, and you use the rehearsal process to revise the text, and maybe whatever visual backup you're using. Then you begin to work on the presentation skills themselves. Where do you want to slow down, speed up, or pause? Where should your voice rise in pitch, where does it fall? What emotions do you feel when telling a personal anecdote? At this point, it's important that you start rehearsing whatever presentation you're giving from beginning to end, without stopping, even if something goes wrong. Remember, when we repeat something over and over, we're training and retraining our nervous systems — and you don't want to train yourself to stop every time something minor goes wrong. Imagine there is an audience present, and figure out how you recover and continue without stopping.

Here's another tip: For the practice of most things, you don't need a mirror or video camera. Once you begin rehearsing, though, you'll find the feedback useful. Video recording is best, with you playing to the camera as though it were your audience. With a mirror, you'll be paying more attention to how you look while you are rehearsing than to your performance, and that will cause you to perform unnaturally. With a recording, you can wait until it's all over before you have a look. The video keeps you honest, and can keep you looking at your performance from the audience's point of view, which provides invaluable feedback.

Finally, with rehearsal, it is almost always helpful to have a director work with you. Steve Jobs didn't rehearse those talks all by himself. He had a coach and a director and a couple of writers working with him the whole time. When we rehearse plays, we have a stage manager and a director working with us at every rehearsal. If you're rehearsing a new project at work, ask your boss to come in and help you perfect it. The director doesn't have to be a professional director, just someone who understands the project you are rehearsing and can lend their point of view and personal knowledge, someone who can provide a "third eye" or different perspective. You'll be amazed at how much faster you can perfect almost anything you care about if you accept the help of that director!

*Chapter 13: The Art of Practice*

## Write Your Own Script

> *"All the world's a stage,*
> *And all the men and women merely players;*
> *They have their exits and their entrances,*
> *And one man in his time plays many parts,*
> *His acts being seven ages."*
>
> Jaques, in William<br>Shakespeare's As You Like It

One of the many ways we mislead ourselves is with the belief that we are either "on," as in on stage, or "off" as in being out of the public eye. We often like to think of ourselves as being "offstage," with no one looking. Unless you're a big-time celebrity with paparazzi tracking your every move, it's understandable that you would feel that way. In that "offstage" persona, we're free not to pay attention to how we look, sound and act.

But in fact, there is almost always someone watching, even beyond your family and friends — and that someone is you. We're always paying attention to ourselves, to who we think we are, who we want to be, and how we're measuring up. And, if we really want to take control of our lives, we might just be choosing to be "on" all the time. We might choose to look and feel and act exactly as we would like to see ourselves all the time.

You may be wondering how this attitude might benefit you, since you're not overtly a performer. The answer is that it will affect virtually everything in your life. You can practice making your breakfast in the morning. How can you make that more efficient, more fun, and wind up eating better? Or perhaps you walk to work. Can you change the pace, and increase your heart rate during the walk? Can you practice awareness of your surroundings while walking or driving? Can you practice the way you greet your fellow workers when you arrive at work? Can you practice the tasks you do at work, consciously so that you get better at them every day? Of course you can.

## Practice for a Better Speaking Voice

Knowing about practice is, of course, only useful if you use it.

Here's one example, drawn from a voice and diction class I took in college. I learned later that it is known as *The Announcer's Test*, originally developed in the early 1940s at Radio Central New York to assess the speaking abilities of prospective radio announcers. It has since become a popular vocal warm-up for voice actors, speakers — and also functions as a memory challenge. If you practice the full test each morning, maybe in the car on your way to work, you'll be developing your voice and speaking ability. This, in turn, will affect how others see you and relate to you. Just try it for two weeks, and see what changes you notice in your world!

Here is the full sequence of the Announcer's Test:
1. One hen
2. Two ducks
3. Three squawking geese
4. Four limerick oysters
5. Five corpulent porpoises
6. Six pairs of Don Alverzo's tweezers
7. Seven thousand Macedonian warriors in full battle array
8. Eight brass monkeys from the ancient, sacred, secret crypts of Egypt
9. Nine sympathetic, apathetic, catatonic old men on roller skates, with a marked propensity toward procrastination and sloth
10. Ten lyrical, spherical, diabolical denizens of the deep who all stall around the corner of the quo of the quay of the quivery, all at the same time.

## Chapter 13: The Art of Practice

The challenge lies in reciting these lines in one breath while maintaining clarity and proper enunciation, making it a favorite among voice actors and performers for practice and warm-up routines. The way I learned it was to start with the first, then take a breath and do the first two, then another breath and do the first three, working all the way up until you can do all ten in a single breath without stumbling or mispronouncing anything.

I've always found this to be most effective as an exercise if I over-enunciate each sound during my practice sessions. That warms up the various facial muscles used to enunciate the sounds. By the time I get through the full sequence, my voice itself and all the muscles needed to create each sound are fully warmed up, and I'm ready to speak more clearly without needing to pay attention to my vocal technique.

It may take you a few days to learn the whole sequence, and a few more before you can do it all in one breath, but when you do, you'll be well on your way to a better speaking voice. If you don't believe having a better voice and speech patterns can change your life, I would invite you to watch the movie "My Fair Lady."

Practice is the secret super power here!

## A Conversation with Jeff McBride

I've known and worked with Jeff McBride for over three decades. I've produced, directed and managed his shows on four continents during that time, in theaters, casino showrooms, and at arts festivals and corporate events around the world. In the following conversations, I particularly wanted to access Jeff's knowledge of the best ways to practice and rehearse for any skill you might wish to develop.

*Tobias Beckwith: Let's talk about the magic of practice and how learning to practice can give you the ability to do things you didn't think you could — maybe even things no one thinks are possible.*

*I know you have stories about you and your dad practicing your magic when you were young, with him checking your angles and coaching you as you did it. Do you want to talk a little bit about how you got started with that?*

*Jeff McBride* : Yes. And I will also say, the concept of practice has changed for me over the years. It's changed because of the teachers that I've encountered. When I didn't have a teacher, I thought practice was something you did to get to an end result, that it wasn't about finding pleasure in the practice, but that the practice was a means to an end, instead of a path towards mastery.

I remember not wanting to practice the first time I was told to practice — it was against my will. My mom called me in on a sunny summer day when I would rather be out turning over rocks in our backyard looking for lizards. She called me into the house, into the dark basement to be chained to a piano like Sybil and forced by a music teacher to learn to play **By the Sea, By the Sea, By the Beautiful Sea** on the piano. It was a painful experience because I really didn't want to be a piano player. I wanted to be a drummer.

Although the piano is a percussion instrument, it wasn't fulfilling my need to hit things. There's a physicality to the drum. So practicing the piano was something that I did not want to do. It was keeping me from other things.

It wasn't until I found magic, conjuring magic, performance magic — that I really understood what practice was. Even with my very first magic book, **The Golden Book of Magic** by the Great Merlini, I didn't read the method. I read the effect and tried to find a way to do it. I didn't know that you had to learn the methodology, the secret workings, in order to be able to successfully put a pencil through a handkerchief. Because it said, "the magician takes a handkerchief and puts a pencil through it." I did not read the entire chapter, so I ruined a lot of handkerchiefs. I didn't know that there was a secret methodology and technique, and that technique had to be learned, then practiced, and then put into practice by performing it. So I was a failure at practice from the get-go. Mostly because I didn't have a teacher.

*Tobias:* Sure.

## Chapter 13: The Art of Practice

*Jeff:* My dad tried his best to work with me. He would watch and tell me when I was doing things incorrectly and would support and congratulate me when I did things right. And so I guess he was my first magic coach, because he wanted me to be great. At least good enough so I wasn't embarrassing when he called me downstairs, "Hey Jeff, the Pearlsteins have come over. Let's do some magic for them." He was proud to show off his kid who did magic. My parents' friends would come over for dinner or for cocktails, and they would invite me to come down and change out of my pajamas into my little magic outfit. And then, you know, at nine years old, 10 years old, I would be performing magic. So I know my dad instilled it in me that I had to practice to get good enough to perform.

*Tobias:* Right. But you started with card manipulation fairly early, didn't you? I remember myself getting the book **Hugard's Card Manipulations** and sitting in my room trying them all, over and over again, and finally decided, "nobody can do this." That changed the first time I saw you do those manipulations in your act, some 20 years later.

*Jeff:* Yes. One of my first magic books was **The Amateur Magician's Handbook** by Henry Hay. It had card manipulation instruction, and particularly card production moves where you would show your hand empty and then a card would appear. I tried this, and I went, "that is impossible!" I didn't do it for a long time because it was so difficult — until I witnessed another person doing it. Suddenly, I realized that, "oh, it *is* possible!" I witnessed a man named Colin Rose, a card manipulator, at a magic show at the Felt Forum at Madison Square Garden, perform a card manipulation act. And then I went back to that book and told myself I could learn to do what he did — because I saw it. It was off the page and moving in real life.

*Tobias:* Yeah.

*Jeff:* I didn't know it was possible. You know, you can read about the ocean and about water, but until you see the ocean, you don't know how vast it is. You can read about something all you want on the printed page. But until you see it in motion, you're lost. It's not real for you.

So when I saw the cards appearing one at a time from the magician's fingertips, that changed everything. I was like, I don't care how long I have to practice, I must do that. And that is what lit the match for me. It was having an exemplar. I still didn't have a teacher, though. No one to teach me the discipline and the joy of practice. For many years I would practice just to get to the results. But it wasn't practice for the joy and expression of practice. Practice for the spiritual path it is in itself.

I remember going to dance class to learn moves to do. I wasn't dancing for the sake of dance and wasn't enjoying the dance. I was a person with a mission — to be able to hit a certain position. It took me a long time, maybe until I met Joshua Levin, who really turned my head around on what practice is. Joshua is an incredible musician, an incredibly disciplined musician who puts in his hours per day, every day. He's a tabla player — a master tabla player — which is one of the most difficult instruments in the world. He was studying at the Ali Akbar College of Music in California. They have a really different kind of attitude about what practice is. There's the idea of being 'in the practice,' of working on your virtuosity and entering a state of musicality that transcends the mundane world and even mundane music.

So these musicians work so hard on these ragas, on these very complex rhythms that put them in an exalted consciousness, some would say a spiritual state, where they're riding on this music, pushing their edges, making it more and more complex and more and more beautiful.

And then the phone rings, and it interrupts their practice. It's a gig at a wedding, which is going to pay the bills for the music studio where they are in the practice of this music. The phone rings, and now they have to pack up all their equipment, transport it across town to the wedding, where people are drinking and not paying attention to the music. It's background. They play their music and try to get into that state they had reached in the studio.

## Chapter 13: The Art of Practice

*Maybe they do. Hopefully they do. Maybe they can turn that party around, but maybe not.*

*When the gig ends, they come back, recalibrate, and now they dive deeper into the practice. So the practice is being equally, if not more, important as a state of consciousness than the actual performance. I don't think that is a common experience in the Western world. There's this idea that, if you practice, you're practicing towards an end, and not for the sake of the practice itself.*

*That changed my experience with my magic, of exploring magic, reading magic, learning magic, because I'm not learning magic anymore for myself and my performances. I'm studying magic for my students. So I study outside my comfort zone. I might have students who are working on really diverse styles of magic that I don't perform. But I want to experience, I want to practice the techniques so I can convey what I experience through these different forms of magic.*

*Tobias: I get that. But how do you inspire your students to practice? Because we all have different levels. One student hates to practice, another loves it. One struggles to put in 10 minutes a day, and another will go on for hours.*

*Jeff: Abigail, my wife, has an incredible story about her learning to play the piano. She's quite a good piano player — a great musician, actually — great drummer, plays keyboards, plays African harp, all these different instruments. I don't think she was enjoying taking some of the lessons — I don't think anybody enjoys being bad at something. We just want to be good at something. We want to get a shortcut, that hack to go beyond those first lessons. So she asked her music teacher, her piano teacher early on, "But how long do I have to practice?" And the music teacher said, "You have to practice until you want to practice."*

*I think that it was the same for me. I had to practice until I learned that I wanted to do it. And now I practice routines and card magic, especially card magic routines that I will maybe never perform for people or will only perform for a very limited group of magicians.*

*I work with Mat Franco. Mat and I both have this passion for card magic. He'll come over and we'll sit down and sit for hours, and he'll perform routines that he will never do on stage or on TV, but that he loves to practice and perform. Because the practice is this therapeutic, reflective state. And there's a beauty to that, surrendering to the practice without that kind of desire to push it out into the world. To kind of retreat from the world into the practice instead of putting it out as performance.*

*And I know that I am just now able, because I've practiced so much, to really trust my intuition in the moment when I'm performing. That's very hard for a magician — to surrender to flow states — because magic, by its nature, is about controlling people's perceptions, controlling actions, sight lines, what they hear, what they say, what they feel, what they experience. And flow states are about surrendering and giving up control into the flow. So there's this dance between control and flow. Now, at 65 years old, I'm finally learning how to merge these two states.*

*It happened just today in an on-line conference. I had not planned to teach this piece of magic with these little heart shaped props. But the conversation led towards sharing love with community while we're in this learning experience. I just jumped into the flow and said, you know, I think I can do this — and it was received warmly. It was all about trusting the practice in order to be able to surrender to the flow.*

*Tobias: That's great. The practice really gets you to that state of, I'm not sure the right word is mastery, but where those skills you've practiced just become a part of your vocabulary of things you can just do.*

*Jeff: It transcends the technique or the self-consciousness censors. Especially for magic, there's always a lot of censorship going on. There's a lot of restrictions with techniques. Jazz musicians can surrender to techniques and make blue notes, and take what other people would call mistakes and turn them into gold. They learn to alchemize these moments where there's all of a sudden a glitch in the technique, but that releases gold.*

## Chapter 13: The Art of Practice

*Tobias:* Whereas the less masterful performer has the technique that glitches, and makes the mistake and thinks, "Damn. I screwed up!"

*Jeff:* Yeah, it's like mastery is never saying "Oops." That's huge.

*Tobias:* I remember you joking that, "Mastery comes when all the things that possibly can go wrong has gone wrong, and you've figured out how to deal with them all."

Let's move on and look at this from a slightly different angle. You have set three Guinness World Records, and they were world records in skills that 99.9% of human beings can't do at all. How did you practice while preparing for that? Because you knew for a month or two that we were going to do that.

*Jeff:* Well, first of all, it was about setting myself an achievable goal, not an unachievable goal. Also, it was, once again, having an exemplar. I had seen this magician, Earl Everett Johnson, whose professional name was Presto. He could roll eight coins on his fingers very gracefully, eight silver coins at once. In the community of magicians in New York City, which is very competitive, just that one flourish established him as the grandmaster of sleight of hand. What I didn't know at the time was that, some say, he had been in jail in his early days, and that was one of the ways he passed the time. How he didn't get the coins taken away is another mystery. However, that was supposedly what happened. He was a great guy, the sweetest guy in the world. But that was the rumor, that he must have been in jail to have had time to perfect this technique.

Well, I didn't have jail, but I did have two years on the road with the Radio City Rockettes, which believe me, was not jail. I was very popular with the entertainment bookers at Radio City Music Hall, which is bizarre because I do a solo act on stage in the largest theater in the world, 6,000 people, with no camera support. But they loved me because I could entertain in these big halls. I think people respected that I had developed the discipline to be able to put a show on in a giant theater with very few props. I could do it because I had studied a lot of different theatrical disciplines. Kabuki theater, mask, mime, dance, magic. And I lived and worked in New York City, so I had to get my entire show into a taxi or it didn't go. So it was survival. I had to be able to pack small and play the biggest theaters in the world.

So Radio City Music Hall takes me on the road with a 100-person show: **The Great Radio City 60th Anniversary Spectacular, starring The Rockettes with Susan Anton and Jeff McBride.** I'm doing two spots in the show, and the show is two and a half hours long. I am backstage every day hours before the show begins, waiting in the wings. Hours waiting to go on. Instead of killing time, I worked it to death. I worked on drills and drills and put hours in every day practicing. Sometimes it was just an insane amount of hours of joyful practice. And it was through those countless hours practicing that I was able to achieve that level of mastery that got me into the **Guinness Book of World Records** three times.

Tobias: Awesome. One of the things we talk about at your school is the difference between practice and rehearsal of a piece that you're doing. I've touched on that a little bit above, but I'd love your particular take on it.

Jeff: Eugene Burger, my teacher for over 30 years, had a great take on this: "Practice the parts, rehearse the whole." You can stop during practice. You can't stop during rehearsal. And one of the things that separates the hack from the master is their ability to navigate all of the bumps and what we would call mistakes in performance. The master is able to make those mistakes disappear or to negotiate those bumps in the most beautiful way — whether dramatically or humorously or with great humility — to be able to move continuously from beginning to end. You move through them all, and the audience doesn't know that anything went wrong. And then you take your final grand bow with a big smile and go back and shut the dressing room door and curse yourself out and knock your head against the wall.

## Chapter 13: The Art of Practice

*Actually, it's being able to move beyond that dressing room self-damnation, to move out into the audience after the show, meet and be able to take stock and learn from it. You learn not to beat yourself and to flagellate yourself because you made mistakes. And that's really hard to do. I see people beating themselves up all the time because they made mistakes.*

*Eugene used to say to performers, "Oh, you get so nervous. If you didn't practice, you **should** be nervous. And if you fail, you should maybe not shrug that off." But if you have practiced and you did the best you could, you just, as my friend Larry Haas teaches us, put your hands on your heart and say, "I did the best I could." And, you know, you have to forgive yourself.*

*Tobias: It's also important that you learn to know the difference between a mistake that you made and want to beat yourself up about, and the mistake that teaches you to improve.*

*Jeff: There's an old wisdom teaching that says there are always three shows: The show you practiced, the show you performed, and the show you should have done. That's the one that keeps you up late at night.*

*Eugene Burger had a wonderful story about practice, performance, and reflection. There he was, Eugene Burger, one of the great close-up performers of our time, performing at the Magic Castle, perhaps the greatest environment for performing magic in the world. Magic lovers, private club, special guests, you have to know a member to get in. He's performing in the very prestigious Close-up Gallery, and someone comes up after his show and says, Eugene, I'm having a party, a birthday party, and I'd love you to come do your show. Eugene asks, what would you want me to do? The guy says, "just what you did here."*

*Now, Eugene was doing his formal close-up act. It was a very formal close-up magic theater act, in a very controlled environment of 30 people on a raked stage, with everyone's entire focus and an MC introducing him. He says, okay. He talks with the client on the phone, the guy sends him the check, and he's on his way to the gig. It was at a marina, which should have given him a clue. He* thought he was to perform in the restaurant at the marina. They said, oh no, the Trevor Plantagenet party is down on Pier 5. He walks down the dock and he realizes this party is on a boat. He hears this this disco music coming out, and this boat has been out at sea all day with the people partying and drinking. Eugene is dressed in a tuxedo, and all these people are in bathing suits and T-shirts. He has this long white beard, and people are starting, as he shows up, to call out, "Hey, Santa's here, dressed in a tuxedo!" and it starts. Eugene was not prepared for that. He did not practice for this particular party.

So he walks in and he's trying to find the host. Everybody is red from being in the sun all day. They're like lobsters — and they're drunk. They're throwing ice cubes at each other. And Eugene all of a sudden has the realization that everybody on the boat is having a great time — except him! Because he was not in the flow of the event with the show he had prepared. So he chose to surrender his expectations of control. He just slipped into the party mind and thought, what if I was one of these party guests? He entered into the flow of the party, and he had a great time entertaining people, meeting them where they were, not where he wanted them to be. He wasn't going to get 30 people sitting in one direction all of a sudden. It was a party. It was a disco party, and it was at the end of the cruise. There's no way. You can't herd cats, you know. So that's an important lesson, to be able to go with the flow. You have to go free-form sometimes and be able to throw away a lot of your expectations of what you think your practice has led you to.

Tobias: Sure. In show business, we learn that that's going to happen more often than we expect, just in the normal course of things. We plan, and we rehearse, and we think it's all ready and going to be great, and then we get a show in front of its first audience. We've forgotten that the audience is half of the experience, and that's something we can't rehearse — except with the audience present.

I remember seeing it happen on Broadway with my first show — **Sweeney Todd**. They rehearsed for three weeks, and I saw every

## Chapter 13: The Art of Practice

rehearsal and I still wasn't quite sure how the show was going to come together. It went in front of the first audience — and they hated it! But Hal Prince, the director, **knew** that the show wasn't going to come together until the audience was there. Both the director, the person putting it all together, and the performers, need that feedback from the audience — and then you rehearse some more. You make changes after every performance, and you rehearse some more. And if you expected it to be perfect for the first audience, you're just going to beat yourself up over something that you shouldn't, you know?

We certainly had that experience with the shows you and I put together, because we did so many different shows and different kinds of shows working together. After opening night, you go back and you take notes and you move things around and you take a piece out and you put a piece in — and after the third or fourth audience, it turns into a great show. But it's seldom a great show the first time. Hopefully, you have enough skill and your team has enough skill, and they've practiced enough that they can now rehearse just once or twice in a new format, and create the show that's perfect.

I didn't know that about Silicon Valley companies before I started hanging out with people there, but the process is similar. They'll tell you to get the 'minimum viable product' to market and see what people think of it. "Oh, we love this thing that was an accident. And we hate the thing that you thought was the main part of the app you built." So you rebuild the product for the users who show up, much as we do with a show in that sense.

But if you don't have the right team, with the skills to rebuild the product overnight, you're screwed. You don't have the skills if they haven't practiced. You don't have a good framework you can tweak if you haven't rehearsed. And that's a big key.

The more I learn about business and organizations, the more I'm aware that the lessons we learn from show business are reflected in each of those other situations. The lessons spill over to personal life in a hundred different ways.

*Maybe I want to go on a date and make specific plans — but then the restaurant turns out to be closed that night, so we have to go somewhere else. Everything that can go wrong, does. You have a choice. Do you want to see it as a terrible date, a wasted evening? Or is it an opportunity to practice your creativity and flexibility? Or maybe it turns out your date isn't the person you thought they were. You can still get to know this person — and maybe that turns into a great friendship, or business contact, or whatever. But having fixed expectations and insisting on them — that screws us up a lot in life.*

That is certainly one of the things I have learned over the years.

I loved your thoughts on the fact that the practice itself becomes the core. We do the things we do because we love to practice them. I remember back when I played a guitar in a band. I really loved playing, and I never had to be told to practice. It was never a chore because I loved playing, for myself or for an audience. My favorite thing was to go to my room with my guitar.

*Jeff:* I learned a lot from Allan Ackerman. And I don't know, one of the interesting things — and this is a secret — is that while we're on this Zoom call right now doing this interview, there's a noise filter, and so you can't hear me shuffling cards. You can't hear this, can you? (Shows cards he has in his hands being shuffled) No. This is a noisy activity that disappears. If I turn my sound filter off, you can hear this, right?

*Tobias:* Sure.

*Jeff:* However, with close-up magic card manipulation, many of its moves and techniques should be hidden and never heard or seen.

*Tobias:* Okay.

*Jeff:* Allan Ackerman, is known as The Las Vegas Card Expert, one of the greatest close-up card experts in the world — you need to be one of the best in the world in order to call yourself The Las Vegas Card Expert. On any Wednesday night, you can go down to the Gary Darwin Magic Club. It's a free magic club in Vegas for

## Chapter 13: The Art of Practice

*the past 55 years. And magicians from all over the world meet with Allan, who is there every week. He helps them, coaches them with their magic. He always has new stuff he's working on.*

*Well, Allan was a math professor at one of the colleges here in Vegas. And he thought that by teaching college, he would have to give up his magic practice. But he learned that if he was teaching five hours a day, he could have that deck of cards just out of sight under his desk while he was teaching. And he could practice — silently, almost unconsciously, working on all of the moves he could do — for five hours a day. He learned how to practice silently and invisibly. The result? He got better than anyone in the world. And he was never self-conscious about his technique because he could be teaching a class on mathematics and basically running computer programs in the background with the cards in his hands. You know what I mean? That same kind of metaphor of things running in the background.*

*So Allan's technique is flawless. It's not self-conscious because he can do it automatically — because he did it for five hours a day, five days a week, all day, every day, for years. And I have taken up that practice. I can be having a conversation — we've been having a conversation here for an hour, and I've been practicing the entire time. And it doesn't distract for one moment or take my focus away, and I'm totally in the flow. So when I take out cards and I go into public now and take them out of hiding and into action, I can be 100% there. I can be 100% with a student or talking — and always just working my practice. I encourage this in people. Don't take it out and practice and be flashy in front of people. But if my hand is in my pocket walking down the street, I can be working on some coin magic. I have all these hours, these little treasures, these pockets of time, and instead of killing time, I can work my craft, my practice, to death.*

*Tobias: That's amazing.*

*One of the things I wanted to talk about is how practice can lead you to the next level in more than one way. When Allan started learning cards, he couldn't have done silent cards under the table* and practiced for hours as you described. First, he had to practice enough just to be able to do the sleights. Then he had to get to a point where they became silent, and then to where he reached the point he didn't have to think consciously about the mechanics. And so you reach different levels as you go.

I know for myself, I remember trying to learn the Downs Palm with a coin, where you put the coin in the crotch of your thumb and you bend your fingers and it comes out between your first and second fingers, and then you flip it out by grabbing it with your thumb. I couldn't do it and I couldn't do it, until I kind of could. But I used to practice it while I was riding on the subway and thought I was no good at it, and no one would ever be fooled — until a guy sitting across from me one day said, "Hey! Where'd the coin go? What are you doing with that coin?" It did get fast enough that I could perform a with it. But later on — years later, actually, I realized I was flipping the coin out the wrong way. I flipped the coin down when I grabbed it — which worked — but it's a lot better if you flip it up! I never would have thought of that if I hadn't practiced the move for a hundred hours before that.

I remember at another point going, "Oh, my fingers don't have to move that much. I can work on having them move a lot less. How can I do it with the hand really hardly moving? You find yourself practicing at a different level.

*Jeff:* Of course, a good coach can correct those things so you don't have to go hundreds of hours or years practicing something the wrong way before you have that realization. There's the saying, "Practice makes perfect," but in reality, only perfect practice makes perfect. That's where the mentors and the coaches come in to shave those years off of your learning curve because you're practicing something wrong. I get students here that say, I can't produce cards. I can't produce cards. I help them make one slight adjustment, and suddenly they're producing cards, and they cannot believe the breakthrough happens within minutes.

I think we can leave it there. Perfect practice makes perfect.

## Chapter 13: The Art of Practice

*Tobias: Exactly, which I touched on earlier, but without that important caveat: Practice with a coach, practice with a teacher. Save yourself that first hundred hours of mistakes and bad practice.*

*Jeff: Take lessons.*

*Tobias: This has been great. Thank you, Jeff!*

## Movement and Memory

As an actor, memorization is a key skill. You're handed a new script, and expected to know your lines very quickly. But for many of us, memorizing long texts is difficult.

I remember a discovery I made back when I was performing in a play as a teenager. Learning the script on my own was tough. Even if I had a partner to run lines with — we would correct each other as we went — it took what seemed like forever. But the minute we started with blocking rehearsals — the ones when you are on a semblance of the set of the play, deciding where you move and when — the memorization became easy. When you sat down, you would say one line. Wave your hand when you said another, and stand up on yet another. Once we combined the lines we were learning with physical actions, it was all suddenly quite easy!

Later on in life, while teaching and directing magicians, I rediscovered the same phenomenon. If a magician created a script and tried to memorize it, they often found it nearly impossible. The result was a performance that was largely improvised, and usually not very good. Once I showed them that each line would match an action, and they should memorize it "on their feet," everything changed. Here's an example.

Come in and accept your applause. As you come up from your little bow, you say — your opening line. Then, turn to your table and pick up prop #1 — and say your second line.

The minute scripted lines became coupled with physical actions, students no longer had difficulty in learning and remembering them.

This same principle works for any kind of presentation. Are you giving a pitch for your new business? Don't read from your slides! Instead, use your blocking, your movement and gestures, to guide your talk. This doesn't mean you can't use slides or other visual aids. But use them to enhance the talk, not as your script.

Let's imagine for a moment that I'm giving a presentation on subjects contained in this book.

After my introduction and initial applause, I say:

Here's a big concept for you. "The reality you experience is just an illusion, created inside your own mind!"

I have to know the beginning of that line without a cue, but as I say "created in your mind," a slide comes up with those words written over an image of a brain. I turn and look at the slide for a moment, and as it fades, I turn back to the audience and say:

Well, not completely within your mind. I'm not saying there's nothing "out there." There is certainly something out there!

I turn to my table onstage and pick up a small sign that says, "Out there."

But how does what's out there, get in here?

I point to the sign, and then to my head.

It comes in through my senses! Sight, sound, touch, taste and smell. They exist to tell me — my mind — what's out there!

As I say "through my senses," I pick up a second sign, smaller than the first, that says "The Senses."

"But as you can see, only part of what's really out there gets in through the senses."

I show that the "senses" sign is smaller than the "out there" sign.

"Our senses are designed for survival, not understanding. Only about 1% of the electromagnetic waves are visible light. We only hear sounds between 20 and 20 thousand megahertz … and it's the same with our other senses."

### Chapter 13: The Art of Practice

As I say that last bit, I gesture with the two signs, and when I remember those gestures, I remember the lines.

I won't lay out the whole talk here, but I hope you're beginning to understand. If I try to use my mind and voice by themselves, it is much more difficult to remember this whole talk than it is when I use props combined with movement. As long as I have the props and move with them, I'll always remember the lines.

By the way, you can try this for yourself. If you've tried learning *The Announcer's Test* from Chapter 3, you probably had trouble memorizing the last few items. Go back and make up movements illustrating those items. Do the movements along with the phrase, and you'll find you can learn them much more quickly!

*The Performer's Edge*

*Conclusion*

# Conclusion

We're nearly done here. Let's take a look at where we've been. The book is essentially about the idea of how reality is created and can be changed. It touches on how performers interact with and shape our perceptions of reality, the role of culture in defining what's real, and how aligning our actions with our beliefs is a key to affecting change. Mahatma Gandhi's quotes have emphasized the importance of taking personal responsibility in creating change, and the quote from William Shakespeare's *As You Like It* highlighted the performative nature of life, and how we all play roles — roles we have the ability to choose for ourselves. The underlying message is that ***we all have agency in constructing our reality*** both individually and collectively.

## Point-by-Point Summary

Here's a breakdown of the book's key ideas:

- **Creating Reality:** The core theme is the fact that our minds are active participants in the creation of reality. It is not something that simply exists, but rather something that is co-constructed by our actions, beliefs, culture and environment.
- **Performers and Reality:** Each of us can use the 'secrets' of performers to shape our perceptions and prompt us to consider different realities. The abilities performers have on stage can translate directly to our individual capabilities to shape the reality we experience.
- **Changing Culture to Change Reality:** Reality is created at both an individual and a cultural level. If we want to change our collective reality, we must change our culture.
- **Responsibility:** We are each responsible for what we want the world to be. Change is not something to wait for from some external source, but something we must create and embody ourselves. When we take the responsibility for the change, we gain the power to make it happen.
- **Aligning Action with Belief:** The way we align our actions

with our beliefs creates and shapes our reality. Intentional alignment between our values and our behaviors is key to the co-creation of our reality.
- **From the Outside In**: Our inner world is reflected in the outer world. That means we create change from within ourselves, and that our external world, in a sense, is a mirror of our own inner world. As performers on the stage that is our reality, we can be imprisoned by our existing emotional experiences, or transform ourselves by choosing to act as the people we need to become, right here, right now.
- **All the World's a Stage:** Shakespeare's quote serves as a reminder that we can view life as a performance. It indicates how we each play different roles throughout our lives. It also underscores how this performance, or our individual actions, shapes the world we experience. It suggests that our 'performance', our actions, choices, roles, shapes the reality that surrounds us.

In essence, I hope we've presented a brief but powerful argument for the idea that *reality is not a fixed entity.* It is a dynamic construct that we actively participate in, and that our intentions, culture, actions and beliefs shape our world and that our world also shapes our inner selves. In other words, we're each more powerful than we have previously imagined.

## Think Different

In his iconic advertising campaign, Steve Jobs urged us to "Think Different." The phrase's apparent grammatical flaw was, in fact, a deliberate choice. It challenged us not merely to alter our thought processes, but to contemplate entirely new concepts. We're being commanded not just to think of different things, but to think in different ways.

This book aims to expand our mental horizons. A key insight came from Donald Hoffman's TED talk, which posits that our perceived reality is largely illusory, constructed from sensory input and shaped by our beliefs and experiences. As a theater practitioner and mentor to

## Conclusion

magicians, I should have recognized this concept earlier, but Hoffman's clarity was revelatory.

Our individual experiences are inextricably linked to our cultural context. We are, in many ways, akin to bees in a hive, believing ourselves to be autonomous while unknowingly contributing to a collective consciousness. This cultural mind shapes our beliefs and, consequently, our perceived reality.

Each one of us possesses the power to alter this illusion we call reality. Just as, in the theater, we create experiences and imagined worlds for our audiences, so can we modify our experience of our "real world." We can change the external, material world through technology and engineering. This seems obvious, but we think less often that we can transform our internal landscape by reshaping our beliefs and acquiring new knowledge, and that our experienced reality is created just as much from knowledge and belief as it is from the inputs we receive through our senses from that external world.

For leaders in business and society, understanding this multifaceted nature of reality creation is crucial for effecting change. When Steve Jobs returned to Apple, his "Here's to the Crazy Ones," campaign wasn't about better computers, *per se*, it was about changing the way we thought about computing as a means of enabling world changers. It's not enough just to have the technology. To create real change in the world, you must change minds.

As a theater director, I've learned that storytelling is a powerful tool for shaping reality. A theatrical production encompasses myriad factors: a story, the script, actors' methods, the venue's characteristics, the audience's expectations. Similarly, in our daily lives, we must be mindful of our desires, our responses, and the contexts in which we operate.

To create meaningful change, we must embrace responsibility for our circumstances and actions. Gandhi's advice to "become the change you wish to see" is a call to action which remains profoundly relevant. This approach, while sometimes indirect, can yield surprising results.

Questioning our assumptions, especially those we've never thought to examine, is vital. Discomfort often signals areas ripe for growth and improvement. Exposure to diverse cultures, whether through literature, film, or travel, can significantly broaden our perspectives and enhance our capacity for change.

In this grand theater of existence, we are simultaneously the playwright, the actor, and the audience. Our stories shape our reality, and our reality shapes our stories. By crafting narratives that challenge, inspire, and illuminate, we can rewrite not just our own lives, but the very fabric of our shared world.

So let us think different. Let us embrace the discomfort of the unknown, for it is in this soil that the seeds of innovation take root. Let us travel across the vast expanses of our own minds, always questioning, always examining the different perspectives available to us. It is there, in the uncharted territories of thought, that we will find the power to transform our world, one beautifully different idea at a time.

*Conclusion*

*The Performer's Edge*

# Index

Ackerman, Allan   200, 201
Acting   5, 35, 88, 138, 139, 140, 141, 142, 148, 151, 153, 154, 177, 216,
Action   10, 27, 28, 30, 43, 46, 47, 51, 57, 61, 71, 101, 105, 110, 118, 129, 131, 140, 144, 145, 147, 151, 159, 160, 164, 170, 173, 175, 183, 194, 201, 203, 207, 208, 209,
Allen, Paul   92
Assumptions   3, 10, 32, 98, 124, 137, 163, 164, 166, 169, 210
Attention   2, 10, 18, 21, 22, 24, 31, 37, 48, 60, 103, 111, 115, 131, 135, 143, 144, 153, 154, 160, 171, 172, 177, 178, 179, 180, 181, 184, 186, 187, 189, 192
Beliefs   1, 3, 6, 7, 9, 10, 16, 24, 29, 31, 32, 34, 35, 51, 53, 54, 57, 80, 113, 129, 131, 144, 156, 158, 160, 161, 162, 163, 171, 187, 207, 208, 209
Boundaries   7, 34, 62, 115, 118, 125,
Bourke-White, Margaret   59
Brallier, Sylvia   13, 130, 171 +
Branson, Richard   181
Burger, Eugene   66, 196, 197,
Change 6, 11, 29, 36, 37, 49, 51, 59, 63, 67, 68, 69, 73, 74, 75, 76, 77, 78, 79, 82, 88, 110, 111, 112, 113, 116, 129, 130, 131, 132, 137, 142, 145, 148, 156, 160, 163, 164, 189, 191, 207, 208, 209
Cheyer, Adam   93
Clinton, Bill   122, 8, 9, 10
Comfort Zone   14, 81, 156, 193

Conscious, consciousness   17, 24, 26, 28, 32, 37, 38, 48, 51, 130, 132, 133, 134, 135, 136, 137, 138, 144, 170, 171, 172, 180, 192, 193, 201, 202, 209,
Copperfield, David   11, 43, 99, 105, 117, 121,
Culture 2, 3, 6, 7, 11, 24, 28, 34, 38, 43, 51, 53, 54, 55, 60, 61, 62, 63, 64, 65, 66, 67, 77, 80, 81, 82, 83, 85, 88, 89, 104, 111, 115, 125, 127, 130, 142, 150, 173, 207, 208, 210
Darwin, Gary   200
Disguise   44, 118
Disillusionment 3, 4, 5, 12, 55, 60
Disney   30, 40, 43, 46, 87, 121, 156
Draper, Paul   10, 12, 23, 24+, 51+, 65+, 99
Einstein   36, 63, 74, 138
Emerson   36, 46
Feynman, Richard   138, 163, 167, 168
Freedom   7, 33, 109
Gandhi, Mohandas   36, 59, 63, 74, 129, 130, 138, 207, 209
Gates, Bill   45, 93, 104
Gatto, Anthony 71
Goals   82, 91, 105, 116, 117, 118, 119, 122, 131, 132, 134, 135, 138, 140, 145, 146, 147, 148, 181, 195
Harris, Paul   57, 58
Hoffman, Donald   16, 208, 209
Houdini, Harry 46, 99, 100
Hypnosis   13, 111, 112, 113, 132, 134, 136

Identity 1, 45, 48, 54
Illusion 2, 3, 5, 6, 10, 11, 12, 13, 16, 23, 30, 31, 35, 37, 39, 40, 42, 43, 46, 51, 52, 53, 54, 55, 56, 57, 58, 60, 105, 121, 167, 183, 204, 209
Jobs, Steve   1, 8, 9, 10, 38, 45, 47, 63, 73, 74, 92, 93, 156, 185, 186, 208, 209
Johnson, Earl Everett   195
Kahneman, Daniel   166
Kee, Viktor   71
Larsen, Milt   83
Lepine, Kevin   13, 111+
London 79, 84, 99, 101, 173, 174
Maven, Max   66
McBride, Jeff   6, 10, 13, 35, 41, 55, 66, 94, 105, 119, 126, 143, 189+
Memory   18, 27, 32, 35, 40, 60, 132, 137, 140, 145, 154, 179, 188, 203
Mindfulness   34, 130, 131, 143, 144, 145
Mission 76, 145, 146, 147, 148, 149, 150, 151, 181, 192
Movement   2, 133, 136, 139, 140, 178, 203, 204, 205
New York   1, 9, 15, 41, 44, 84, 85, 119, 154, 173, 174, 188, 195, 196
Olivier, Lawrence   141
Perception   23, 24, 25, 26, 27, 29, 31, 32, 33, 34, 35, 37, 40, 42, 47, 49, 53, 111, 137, 194, 207
Practice 5, 13, 21, 63, 99, 101, 103, 105, 132, 139, 143, 144, 183, 184, 185, 186, 187, 188, 189, 190, 191, 192, 193, 194, 195, 196, 197, 198, 199, 200, 201, 202, 203
Reality   3, 6, 8, 9, 10, 11, 12, 15, 16, 17, 18, 19, 21, 22, 23, 24, 25, 26, 27, 28, 29, 30, 31, 32, 33, 34, 35, 36, 39, 40, 46, 47, 48, 49, 51, 53, 56, 57, 58, 65, 66, 72, 93, 131, 133, 136, 153, 158, 163, 164, 166, 167, 169, 170, 173, 175, 202, 204, 207, 208, 209, 210
Rehearsal   13, 174, 184, 185, 186, 196, 199
Responsibility   7, 13, 109, 110, 111, 112, 113, 115, 116, 117, 118, 119, 121, 122, 124, 126, 127, 148, 207, 209
Robbins, Tom   8, 55
Robbins, Tony   118
Scotland Yard   99, 100
Senses   3, 15, 16, 17, 18, 25, 28, 29, 34, 132, 204, 209
Shakespeare, William   90, 173
Story   2, 11, 18, 37, 41, 46, 48, 52, 57, 59, 60, 65, 66, 67, 68, 69, 70, 71, 72, 73, 74, 75, 76, 78, 78, 80, 82, 83, 84, 85, 86, 87, 88, 89, 90, 91, 92, 98, 99, 101, 113, 119, 125, 133, 134, 142, 158, 178, 180, 183, 193, 197, 209
Subconscious   28, 37, 38, 41, 132, 133, 134, 135, 136, 140, 146, 154, 170, 171, 172
Tempest, Marco 10, 15, 26, 47, 94, 119, 123
Trance   13, 37, 58, 65, 85, 132, 133, 134, 137
Value   3, 41, 42, 51, 52, 53, 54, 55, 73, 88, 120, 123, 126, 130, 144, 149, 168, 208
Verities   130
Vitale, Joe   65, 133
Wozniak   92
Zander, Benjamin   110

*INDEX*

# Acknowledgments

Special thanks to my collaborators, Sylvia Brallier, Paul Draper, Kevin Lepine and Jeff McBride for participating, and for all the thoughtful discussions we had. You made the writing of this book a joyful experience, and helped me stretch the bounds of my own thinking.

A special thanks to Sylvia Brallier for her invaluable insights and great work helping me to edit and format the book! Sylvia also created the great illustrations for the sections teaching simple magic tricks. You can see more of her artwork at *www.sylviabrallierart.com*.

# Follow Up

## Other Books by Tobias Beckwith

### For Business Leaders

### The Wizard's Way: Secrets from Wizards of the Past Revealed for World Changers of Today

*This book examines more ways of "Thinking Different," but instead of drawing from the world of actors and magicians, it uses thinking and stories from the real wizards of our world, including Steve Jobs, Mohandas Gandhi, Albert Einstein, Eve Ensler and Leonardo da Vinci.*

### The Wizards Way to Powerful Presentations

*Too many would be leaders in business, though brilliant when it comes to understanding the technology and operations of their businesses, fail as communicators. This book seeks to remedy that.*

### For Magicians and other Performers

### Beyond Applause: Marketing & Management for Independent Performers

*For those performers seeking to become professional, or to improve their businesses as professional entertainers. Marketing, finance, legal, and much more. Derived from Tobias' 40 years managing performers and shows in many different markets.*

## Beyond Deception, Vols 1 & 2

*Two books for magicians exploring ways they can become better performers by developing creativity and performance skills, much of which is derived by applying skills Tobias learned while studying and teaching acting and directing.*

*All of the above are available on Amazon*

### Learn more at our web sites:

*www.triplemusepublications.com*

*www.tobiasbeckwith.com*

*www.yourmagic.com*

*www.wizardventure.com*

### And for:

**Sylvia Brallier:** *www.sylviabrallierart.com*

**Paul Draper:** *www.pauldraper.com*

**Kevin Lepine:** *www.hypnosisunleashed.com*

**Jeff McBride:** *www.mcbridemagic.com*